Mrs. Magavero

A History Based on the Career of an Academic Librarian

Mrs. Magavero

A History Based on the Career of an Academic Librarian

BY

JANE BRODSKY FITZPATRICK

Library Juice Press, LLC
Duluth, Minnesota

Copyright Jane Brodsky Fitzpatrick, 2007
Oral history interview copyright Jane Brodsky Fitzpatrick and Filomena Magavero, 2005

Published by Library Juice Press
P.O. Box 3320
Duluth, MN 55803
http://libraryjuicepress.com/

Library Juice Press is an imprint of Litwin Books, LLC.

This book is printed on acid-free paper that meets all present ANSI standards for archival preservation.

Text design by Rory Litwin
Cover design by Topher McCulloch

Library of Congress Cataloging-in-Publication Data

Fitzpatrick, Jane Brodsky.
  Mrs. Magavero : a history based on the career of an academic librarian / by Jane Brodsky Fitzpatrick.
     p. cm.
  Includes bibliographical references.
  ISBN 978-0-9778617-5-0 (acid-free paper)
  1. Magavero, Filomena I., 1922- 2. Academic librarians--United States--Biography. 3. Women librarians--United States--Biography. 4. State University of New York Maritime College--Professional staff--Biography. 5. Women in library science--United States. 6. Sex discrimination in employment--United States. I. Title.
  Z720.M195F58 2007
  020.92--dc22
  [B]
                                               2007046349

ACKNOWLEDGMENTS

I am grateful to Richard H. Corson, Librarian at the Maritime College for almost forty years, and mentor, whose encouragement, wit, and example exposed me to the best standards to which a librarian can aspire. His knowledge and dedication to the college and the Stephen B. Luce Library has set a high standard for all of us who worked with him.

I would also like to thank Julie Cunningham, Chief Librarian at The Graduate Center, City University of New York, for allowing me the time to pursue my Master's Degree. Thank you to the Interlibrary Loan staff at the Graduate Center, for providing, in a timely manner the multitude of articles from long ago and far away. My adviser, Rachel Brownstein, was a great help to me and responded always in an incredibly timely manner with suggestions which enabled me to hone and clarify my thesis.

And last, but certainly not least, thanks to Filomena Magavero, whose stories, determination and dedication are an important part of the story of women in library history. Fil, thank you for the great meals and the illuminating narrative.

CONTENTS

Acknowledgments	v.
Contents	vii.
Preface	ix.
Introduction	1.
Women in Library History	5.
The Maritime Colleges	41.
Mrs. Magavero	47.
Conclusion	57.
Afterword	61.
Transcript of Oral History	63.
Bibliography	83.

PREFACE
By Susan Searing

This study, based on a lively and readable interview, is a welcome contribution to both women's history and library history. In recent decades library historians have paid considerable attention to gender and use varied methodologies to illuminate the working lives of 20th-century women librarians. Biographies of high achievers like Katharine Sharp and Anne Carroll Moore spotlight individual contributions to the advancement of the profession. Other scholars look at women in the aggregate; numerous statistical studies document the relatively low status of women in the field over time. Since the 1970s, feminist librarians have been vocal in pinpointing discriminatory practices and agitating for equal rights. Still under-represented in the literature, however, are insights into the day-to-day experiences of women librarians who never ascended to positions of power and influence, who did not shake up the establishment, but who performed their assigned duties with skill and dedication and found intangible rewards in the work itself. Their titles and paychecks failed to reflect their true worth as employees, and they suffered persistent humiliations—from being burdened with clerical duties to seeing desired promotions given to men with fewer qualifications. Yet they soldiered on with good humor. The story of "Mrs. Magavero" enriches our understanding of what many female librarians faced on the job during the second half of the 20th century.

Jane Brodsky Fitzpatrick thoroughly contextualizes Filomena Magavero's experiences by portraying the dual reality of the library profession and the maritime academies of her day. Isolated as the only woman professional in an all-male environment, long before second wave feminism took root within librarianship, she was perceived as a clerk by the library's users and her colleagues, although her educational credentials in many cases exceeded theirs. In establishing nurturing relationships with young male students, she fulfilled their expectations that a woman would provide comfort and advice. The sex discrimination to which she was subjected is not diminished by the fact that she found the work and the relationships supremely rewarding and happily endured long commutes to continue on the job. Magavero's mistreatment by her male superiors and colleagues at the New York Maritime College is chilling precisely because it was so ordinary. Searching for an explanation, she concludes that "they were mean, that's the word that comes to mind all the time." But as Fitzpatrick makes clear, it was not merely personal animosity at play, but rather the patriarchal culture of the institution. Magavero's experiences as a woman professional were echoed in thousands of workplaces in that era, although sex discrimination may have been manifested more subtly in other library settings where women were able to support each other.

Magavero faults herself for neither leaving nor fighting to better her situation, but Fitzpatrick convincingly absolves her from blame. How sad, nonetheless, that this hard-working and selfless librarian looks back from retirement and states repeatedly that she regrets not being more assertive in demanding fair treatment. "Maybe I did a disservice to the profession," she worries aloud. Magavero is a survivor. The laughter that so frequently punctuates the oral history transcript is testimony to her irrepressible spirit. I wish I knew Fil Magavero personally. I'm so grateful to Jane Fitzpatrick for sharing her friend with us in these pages.

INTRODUCTION

I worked with Filomena Magavero for ten years, at the Stephen B. Luce Library at the State University of New York (SUNY) Maritime College. Although she was officially retired by the time I began work at Maritime, in 1994, she was still commuting from the northwest Bronx to the extreme southeast Throg's (sometimes spelled Throgg's) Neck Peninsula, a long trip on public transportation, working one day a week as the volunteer government documents librarian. Because of her experience and special knowledge (she had been instrumental in establishing the archives at the Luce Library), she was also the reference contact for most archival questions, dealing mainly, but not solely, with the history of the Maritime College at Fort Schuyler, in her beloved Bronx, New York.

For years, I would give Fil (known to almost everyone as "Mrs. Magavero") a ride to the subway on my way home, and she would repay me by taking me to many wonderful restaurants. During those dinners, she recounted her experiences at Maritime during the 1950s and 60s. I told her she should create an oral history about her unique experiences in the macho culture of the maritime community (both academic and professional), but she always dismissed the idea.

Fil finally fully retired in 2003, and I left the Maritime College in 2004. When I enrolled in an oral history class in the City University of New York (CUNY) Graduate Center's Continuing Education Program in 2005, I decided to ask her to be my storyteller. I was pleasantly surprised by her immediate enthusiastic reply in the affirmative and set up an interview at the StoryCorps booth in Grand Central Terminal in New York City on November 3, 2005. These oral histories will be indexed and digitally preserved in the Archive of Folk Culture at the Library of Congress. They will be publicly accessible at the American Folk Life Center on the Library's website.

Fil never acknowledged her pioneering role as the only professional woman at Maritime until the mid-1970s. I was surprised when she told me that she regretted that she had not fought harder, that she felt that perhaps she had not served the library profession well by accepting "mean" and discriminatory treatment from the all-male faculty: "As I said in some ways I feel that maybe I did a disservice to the profession, because had I been…you know more of an activist, had I been more forceful, and…not demanding, but in speaking out about what I wanted, it might have made things easier for other librarians, but I didn't do it" (Magavero 80). But neither the library profession nor society as a whole, during her first two decades at the college, offered any encouragement or support for equal pay or better status.

What follows is a review of the library literature, articles, surveys and studies by librarians in journals, books and dissertations, focusing on the years Magavero worked at Maritime, followed by a brief history of the Maritime College. Placing the oral history in the context of what was occurring in the library profession at the time, with comparisons to the other five state maritime academies and the U.S. (Federal) Merchant Marine Academy, I will demonstrate that women librarians were in fact a "Disadvantaged Majority" (Schiller "Disadvantaged Majority").

In her oral history Magavero says, "In a way I think I did an injustice to the profession—not only to myself, but to the profession. Because I wasn't an activist I really didn't know how to handle those guys" (67). The fact is she had no friends and no moral support on campus. Because there was no money for travel, she had no avenue for connections with other librarians, and therefore was like so many women who "lacked good models to encourage their choice of a career in academia" (Tarr 23). Even if Magavero had traveled to conferences, such as the annual American Library Association (ALA) convention, she would not have experienced any serious attention focused on women's issues until the mid-1970s.

Moreover, there was little or no library literature or research focusing on women in the profession, especially surprising when one considers both the preponderance of women in the profession, and also the number of library journals. What *was* written dealt mainly with public librarians, because more women were school (kindergarten through 12th grade) and public librarians and were a minority in academic libraries. Women were more prominent in the lower-status libraries and less likely to advance to positions of leadership in academic (higher-status) libraries. In 1970, only seventeen percent of all librarians worked in academic libraries and fifteen percent in special libraries (SUNY Maritime, although classed as an academic library, has many of the qualities of a specialized library). While women comprised ninety-three percent of school librarians, they were just sixty-six percent of all academic librarians. Furthermore, as Susan Tarr noted in 1973, "About 33% of academic librarians are men, while men make up only 20% of the profession generally" (22). Ninety-two percent of large academic library administrators were male, while sixty-three percent of school library heads were female (Cooper 328). So despite women's prevalence in the profession as a whole, they were a minority in academic libraries, and in administrative positions in those libraries. The larger the university library, the less likely it was for a women to be in charge.

I will examine the literature that Filomena Magavero might have been exposed to and demonstrate that it would have been unlikely for her to have advanced further, or been more accepted, especially at New York Maritime. Examining the library profession from a feminist standpoint for the period roughly corresponding to Magavero's career (1949 to 2003) will add to the history of women librarians in the middle of the twentieth century in the United States. With the Second Wave of feminism came an expansion of research into women's history which produced an entirely new method of discovering and understanding women in history. The major texts which redefined historic methodologies from a feminist standpoint were followed by books written by Heilbrun, Conway, Hildenbrand and others. But these were not published until the late 1980s and early 1990s.

While some of the literature examined in this paper suggests the necessity for such a reexamination, or new examination, of the history of women in libraries, it simply did not exist as a movement which could have had an impact for Magavero for most of her career. In exploring these issues, I will illustrate how difficult Filomena Magavero's situation was at the Maritime College, especially in her first two decades there, and how courageous, and not cowardly, it was for her to stay as long as she did.

WOMEN IN LIBRARY HISTORY

The dearth of research on women librarians underscores the particular position of Filomena Magavero, especially in her early years at the library at SUNY Maritime College, when it was called the New York State Maritime College. A historical overview, *The Role of Women in Librarianship, 1876-1976: The Entry, Advancement, and Struggle for Equalization in One Profession* (Weibel, McCook and Ellsworth) was published in 1979. Not until 1982 did Katherine Phenix, a public librarian, begin to compile biannual "dot-matrix printed bibliographies" for the American Library Association (ALA) (Phenix 170). The first detailed bibliography in book form, *On Account of Sex: An Annotated Bibliography on the Status of Women in Librarianship, 1977-1981*, was published in 1984 (Heim and Phenix). In 1985, Phenix discovered that "Collectively, the Weibel, Heim, and Phenix sources contain approximately 2100 citations. In *Role of Women*, the first 100 years are represented by just over 1000 citations" (170). These titles, published between 1979 and 1984, represent the first scholarly research to uncover and publish women's library history, more than thirty years after Magavero graduated from library school. A perusal of the bibliography at the end of this thesis confirms that scholarly research about women in libraries did not appear much before 1968; of all the references, fewer than ten percent were written before that date.

Before examining the unique aspects of Filomena Magavero's career, including a brief description of maritime education and maritime libraries, it is important to review library literature to understand women and librarianship from the middle to the end of the twentieth century. In 1976, Anne E. Brugh and Benjamin R. Beede, librarians at

Rutgers, The State University of New Jersey, surveyed library literature from 1970 through 1975, in the middle of Magavero's career. At this time, men were being solicited as library administrators to raise the status, and therefore the salaries, of librarians. In 1930, women comprised ninety percent of all librarians (Auerbach 1). The number of male librarians quadrupled between 1930 and 1960 (Schiller *Characteristics* 11), and there was an eighty percent increase in the number of male librarians between 1960 and 1970, according the U.S. Census data cited by Schiller (*Characteristics* 12).

Magavero was hired in 1949, four years before Simone de Beauvoir's *The Second Sex* would be published in an English translation and fourteen years before Betty Friedan's *The Feminine Mystique* appeared and sparked a new wave of feminist activism. Simone de Beauvoir famously wrote, "One is not born, but rather becomes, a woman. No biological, psychological, or economic fate determines the figure that the human female presents in society: it is civilization as a whole that produces this creature...which is described as feminine." (249) She rejected the concept of "woman" as simply a term to designate "not a man," or "other," and thereby set the stage for what the Second Wave feminists would call consciousness raising. She declared that, beyond simply demanding rights, she wanted to write a book that would enable women to dethrone the myth of femininity (Introduction xxix). Beauvoir's work was not so much a call to action as a call to rewrite and rethink the discourse, and in that way to recreate women's self-consciousness.

Betty Friedan's *The Feminine Mystique* was published in 1963, the same year that The Equal Pay Act (Public Law 88-38) was passed by Congress. Ironically, the education that First Wave Feminists and their predecessors had fought so hard for was being put to little use. Friedan discovered the "problem that has no name," the ennui of so many women who went to college yet who ended up married with children, isolated in suburbia, and not working outside the home. "Executive, administrative and professional employees," which would include librarians, were not protected by this law until it was amended in 1972, by Title IX Higher Education Amendments (Tarr 29). When the Civil Rights Act (Public Law 82-352, 78 Stat. 241) was passed in 1964 the word "sex" was added to the text, barring discrimination based on sex along with race, color, religion, and national origin. Although many have claimed that this was actually a strategy to kill the bill, Democrat Representative Howard W. Smith, of Virginia, who inserted the term into the bill, denied that was his intention (NARA). This legislation occurred at the beginning of the Second Wave of feminism, which would deeply and radically change the world. And while feminism has changed and evolved from its middle-class white roots in the 1960s to a multi-cultural, multi-gendered, international movement in the 21st century, it took a longer time for feminism to penetrate the maritime industry and the maritime colleges than it did in to reach the library profession.

Women gained the vote in the United States when the Nineteenth Amendment to the Constitution was ratified in 1920, but World War I had ended the First Wave of feminism, which took a back seat to patriotism and the nationalism of the war effort. Searching through history, historian Joan Kelly observed that feminist women seemed scarce, and that when they appeared, "their ideas seem isolated, separated from each other and from us by long periods of silence and inactivity" (66). It was not until the Second Wave, in the 1960s, that women would again become involved in a fight for rights and equality.

When Fil said, "Had I been more of an activist and if I had spoken out for what I wanted, it may have made things easier for other librarians," (75) my reaction was that she lacked any support system for such outspokenness. SUNYLA, the SUNY librarians' association, was not formed until1969, twenty years after Fil had started at Maritime. Because, as she noted in her oral history, there was no travel money available, she was never able to attend library conferences, such as the annual American Library Association (ALA) meetings, and therefore had little or no communication with other librarians, even within SUNY or with nearby City University of New York (CUNY) librarians. ALA did not begin to address the issue of discrimination against women seriously until 1969, and literature and research on women in academic libraries was scarce. Wanda Auerbach's 1972 article, "Discrimination Against Women in the Academic Library," succinctly encapsulated the problem: "When it comes to information on sex distinctions and patterns within the academic library in particular, there is a virtual absence of material in the journals. *This is in itself diagnostic"* (emphasis mine) (7).

Laurel Grotzinger, in her essay on biographical research, discussed the importance and purpose of biographical studies as a tool that "brings to life the essence of the individual as placed within the framework of a society, a profession, and a universe at a point in time" (139). Even when women were studied, women librarians, or librarians as a whole, were not selected or included. Library history was written by men and about men. Grotzinger's detailed examination of biographical research and studies found a "paucity" of data and an exclusion of women, especially librarians, in every type of publication, from directories to journal articles to bibliographies. As one glaring example, she cited *Notable American Women: The Modern Period* (James and Sicherman), which included women who died between the years 1950 and 1975, and the 1980 supplement (Sicherman and Green): "it is a continuing indication of the nonrecognition of the profession and its women that only 4 of the 442 entries in the 1980 volume are librarians" (144). Grotzinger discovered that a "preponderance of biographical and autobiographical material" was about male librarians (147).

This raises the question whether women were ignored because they did not hold positions of power or because their work was devalued. While women librarians' salaries were low, so were the salaries for women in other professions, and library salaries in general were (and are) also relatively low. Is the work of librarians devalued because women perform it and therefore keep it a "semi-profession" (Brugh and Beede), a term coined by Etzioni in 1969 (Grimm and Stern 694)? Librarianship is often discussed along with nursing, teaching, and social work as feminized professions. While all had initially been male-dominated, as educational opportunities became available to women, they entered these professions, which

> drew on years of socialization and a consciousness bred to serve. They fitted the demand for personal satisfaction, yet met the criteria for women's work. They were careers in the sense that they paid relatively steady salaries…but they explicitly limited possibilities for advancement. (Kessler-Harris 235)

In 1949, eight months after Filomena Magavero began working at the New York State Maritime College, Ralph Munn wrote his controversial article which "re-examine[d] the traditional belief that librarianship needs more and more men within its ranks" (1639). Munn argued that recruiting men for the sole purpose of increasing salaries in the entire profession would only dilute the quality of librarianship and would result in mediocre cohorts. He asserted that, according to library directors, male applicants had "no special interest in libraries or public service." Furthermore, according to Munn, these men were interested solely in secure, well-paying jobs; their "cultural" background was lacking; and they had gone to college simply because of the G.I. Bill.

While this observation may have been true, it merely underscores the essentialist point of view that women are more service-oriented and self-sacrificing to the point of being willing to work for lower salaries as a consequence of sheer dedication to the profession. Munn did admit that a "decent standard of living is essential to all of us," i.e., not just men. Having surveyed library positions and salaries, he maintained that "a single woman without dependents" could in fact live on the low end of the salary range, $4000 a year, and with that would be able to obtain "the necessities and a few of the frills of the living." [Magavero took her second cataloging job, at Hunter College, in about 1948 for what she described as the "monumentally high" salary of $1800 a year (65).] A man with a family would not, however, fare well at this salary level. Munn argued that the low salary meant that men with families would be "so concerned with Junior's need of a winter coat that they [could] bring no enthusiasm or creative thought to their jobs." He then concluded that although the ideal situation would be higher salaries, such was a "wholly unrealistic" expectation. Munn maintained that the influx of men would further degrade women's salaries because women would not obtain the higher positions once men were hired. His conclusion was that "superior women" would not then be attracted to the profession if men were to "secure" the most "attractive" positions, because men were "preferred" by the "governing authorities." Therefore the profession "should be kept attractive to the ablest of women" (1639-40).

In February 1950, John R. Banister rebutted Munn, accepting none of his premises. Banister argued that recruitment does not affect the result of graduation in a profession. He also argued that women often enter professions as "a stop-gap to marriage," while men "usually enter a profession in a serious frame of mind, realizing that it will mean the bread and butter for a lifetime." Banister contended that the $4000 to $5000 annual salary range was not particularly low, and that it was within the range of many other professions which were not plagued by mediocrity as a result. He did acknowledge that female librarians were not necessarily all single, nor were they working for "frills," but for the necessities for themselves and/or for their families (Banister).

The total number of male librarians in the profession did increase, but women remained a majority. Not only was it unfair to women to recruit men in this way, but women would not gain either status or increased salary by recruiting men. The Bureau of Labor Statistics' (BLS) 1975 study of employment in libraries not only revealed the preponderance of women, but also exposed the "negative influence" that the "feminine image" had on librarianship, which resulted in the encouragement of men for administrative (i.e. leadership) positions (Brugh and Beede 944). A brief article in *Library Journal* in 1976 noted that "the number of women in leadership positions is steadily decreasing," continuing a trend from the 1960s, as women directors were replaced by men ("Losses in Directorships for Women Pegged").

This lack of progress is an example of Joan Kelly-Gadol's interpretation of women's history. Kelly-Gadol maintained that women's history is not a progressive one, and that progress for women does not necessarily follow advances for men. Instead, women's history is plagued with regression and backlash. "To take the emancipation of women as a vantage point is to discover that events that further the historical development of men, liberating them from natural, social, or ideological constraints, have quite different, even opposite, effects upon women" (76). The goals of a reexamination of history from a feminist standpoint were to discover examples of women whose achievements were based on their knowledge, intelligence, and accomplishments. Beginning with Christine de Pizan's fourteenth-century writings, Kelly traced women's history through the centuries as women's rights and independence were eroded. In the chapter entitled "Early Feminist Theory and the *Querelle des Femmes*, 1400-1789," she described how European women lost inheritance rights, and were eventually excluded from military, financial, and juridical arenas, as these areas became state functions and men took over the positions of power (85). The concept of chivalry, reducing women to "ladylike" creatures, led to their exclusion from arenas in which they had once actively participated. In short, women did *not* reap benefits from the Renaissance.

Nineteenth- and early twentieth-century feminists often reverted to essentialist arguments that women were innately, or essentially, more virtuous, nurturing and peace loving, and would thereby create a better world given the chance. Suffragist Elizabeth Cady Stanton, along with other activists at the first Woman's Rights Convention in Seneca Falls, New York in 1848, believed that women were by nature different from men, and that because of this difference, women's political activism would create a more just world, a world that would be better for all human beings.

When Simone de Beauvoir declared that one is not born, but rather becomes a woman, it was a radical departure from essentialist thinking that one's biological sex determined one's thought processes, and predetermined one's role in society. Although others before her had argued that biology was not destiny, Beauvoir reasoned that not only did women's lives not have to be determined by biology, but also that the idea of woman, or gender, was a social and cultural construct that could be changed by a new consciousness. She wrote that while a "man" is seen as the universal, as a way of saying a "human being," the use of the term "woman" is limiting. She asked the question why, if ovaries and uterus define woman, man is not also defined by his glands? By positing male as objective, female thus becomes subjective: "He is the Subject...she is the Other" (Introduction xvii).

Feminism has evolved, and feminist history seeks to study women as active agents of their own lives, rather than as beings predestined by biology. But early descriptions of librarians followed just such essentialist thinking. Melvil Dewey's "frail" woman, lacking strength and stamina, would never be able to rise to the same levels as men. In an 1886 speech entitled "Women in libraries: how they are handicapped," Dewey was patronizing and paternalistic. Although he cannot be judged by feminist standards that did not then exist, his words were a reflection of the difficulties that women would encounter.

Carolyn Heilbrun's *Writing a Woman's Life* (1988) was a groundbreaking book which changed the way women's history was read and understood. Heilbrun, considered the mother of modern feminism by many feminist scholars, emphasized the importance of studying women's lives from a different standpoint, treating women as active agents of their own lives, and not as people whose accomplishments are merely the result of happenstance, or of just being in the right place at the right time. Heilbrun proposed a new way of reading, writing, and interpreting women's biographies and autobiographies. Using examples of women writers, including Virginia Woolf, the intellectual mother of the First Wave of feminism, Heilbrun examined how these women, and their biographers, suppressed their true feelings and experiences by following the traditional male patterns of narration and storytelling. *Writing a Woman's Life* reexamined the lives of women from a feminist viewpoint, proposing the use of uniquely female experiences that had been either disregarded or overlooked. Heilbrun believed that women's stories must be examined from outside the traditional patriarchal culture, adding a personal context to biography and autobiography, because without models, "these women are therefore unable to write exemplary lives: they do not dare to offer themselves as models, but only as exceptions..."(Heilbrun 25). If Magavero had understood her situation from such a viewpoint, she might have realized that her circumstances at Maritime were not her "fault," and that she did not have the tools, the voice or the support of others with which to fight macho-ism and sexism, formidable obstacles to overcome. When she decided to just "take it" and "ignore" the men on the faculty, she really was unintentionally suppressing anger, as described by Heilbrun: "in the old genre of female autobiography, which tends...to transform rage into spiritual acceptance" as "what has been forbidden to women is anger" (12,13).

Heilbrun's hypothesis was that women's history had to be told using women's lives as examples, that to understand women's history, one had to reevaluate stories from a woman's point of view. The Second Wave feminists did just that, going back in history to find stories about and by women, stories that had been ignored or written out of history. Jill Ker Conway emphasized the importance of agency in *Written by Herself: Autobiographies of American Women: an Anthology*, using autobiographical writings of women from the nineteenth and twentieth centuries. (Conway became the first woman president of Smith College, but not until 1975, even though Smith was founded as a woman's college in 1871.) Like Heilbrun, Conway wrote that traditional male narratives like *The Odyssey* were not an appropriate model for women's stories. Conway's anthology "shows us the individuals grappling with the problems of describing a life which can't be crammed into conventional categories" such as "bourgeois romances" or "heroic journeys." Women tended to adopt a passive voice, portraying themselves as "women to whom things happened rather than people who shaped events" (Introduction x). Not until the feminist movement in the 1960s and 1970s did women begin to write unromanticized stories in a "new tone of voice, politically aware, energized by rage" (Introduction, xi). Magavero's regrets at having endured sexism and exclusion in silence or helplessness are directly related to this lack of an angry model to follow. Although she was inside the academy, she was more like Virginia Woolf's "daughters of educated men" in *Three Guineas* (1938), who were unable to penetrate the political or academic worlds and were unable to earn good salaries. Opportunities were limited, and women were left on the outside looking in. Woolf, too, was looking for women's narratives, both in *Three Guineas* and in the later *A Room of One's Own* (1928), which became a basic document for Second Wave feminists: "…and I thought…of the shut doors of the library; and I thought how unpleasant it is to be locked out…and of the effect of tradition and of the lack of tradition upon the mind of a writer" (24).

It took women to rediscover women in history, and while discoveries of women's history continue, there was little if any available to a general reader in the 1950's, or even the early 1960's. The title of Suzanne Hildenbrand's anthology *Reclaiming the American Library Past: Writing the Women In* is a perfect example of this type of historical rediscovery, yet it was not published until 1996. Anita Schiller's 1970 article "The Disadvantaged Majority: Women Employed in Libraries" was a call to action, throwing down the gauntlet to the ALA to take the lead in acknowledging and abolishing discrimination against women in the library profession. Published in *American Libraries*, the official publication for ALA members, it would have been widely read. Schiller complained that the "library profession has remained remarkably aloof from this matter" ("Disadvantaged Majority" 345). She also criticized the "do-nothing policy" as an "implicitly desired goal of the present policy of the American Library Association" to discourage women, and encourage men, to enter the library profession ("Disadvantaged Majority" 346). Schiller called for the ALA to pass a resolution to commit to equal opportunities for women in librarianship and to conduct research into the status of women in the library profession. Schiller proposed seven action items in all, but it was not until 1976 that the ALA followed through on her demands. If it took so long for sex discrimination in librarianship to be openly acknowledged on a national scale, imagine the impossibility of redressing sexism on the all-male Maritime College campus.

The first book-length study of women in libraries was Dee Garrison's 1979 *Apostles of Culture: the Public Librarian and American Society, 1876-1920*. Garrison's historical study, although focused on public librarians, was the first to define the "feminization" of the profession. The book covers the period from 1876, the year the ALA was founded, to 1920; therefore, it provides a historical foundation, but does not contain data specifically applicable to Magavero's career at an academic institution since Garrison focused on public libraries. But many of her conclusions, although disputed by some authors, remain valid as overall descriptions of librarianship.

Garrison began by describing the patrician, white middle-class Protestant roots of librarianship. She questioned the altruistic interpretation of library history, that librarians were inspired by the concepts of universal education and Jacksonian democracy (Introduction xiv). Instead, she contended that the upper class felt threatened by the growth of "labor unrest and mass discontent," and she set out to prove that public libraries were formed instead "as a means of arresting lower-class alienation from traditional culture." She continues: "It is important to consider that the building of public libraries was motivated by a fear of egalitarianism and upheaval from below as much as by a desire for democratic extension of education." She described public libraries as "sanitized, feminized, middle-class" environments (Introduction xii-xiii).

Garrison did not disparage the dedication of those who entered the profession so much as she felt that they were limited by their own class backgrounds. She attributed the stereotype of the female librarian as the "grim, prim spinster" and "hostess" of the library to those class roots. The librarians combined a "romantic," "missionary" sense with "cultural arrogance." Most importantly to this thesis, Garrison pinpointed the roots of this lasting stereotype:

> The majority of early women librarians are best understood as true believers in that sexual ideology, essentially antifeminist in tone, which so thoroughly dominated public thought at the turn of the century. They

> were not seriously or openly critical of the belief that the goals and capacities of women were inherently limited in the working world....A natural extension of the nineteenth-century library heritage was the self-image of the second and third generations of the library women: the idealistic servant, the militant maid, the 'modern librarian' of the Protestant progressive period. (xiv)

Thus Garrison embarked on her study to demonstrate that, based on the social mores at the turn of the twentieth century, library leaders contributed to the "feminization" of the library profession that Filomena Magavero was to enter in the middle of the century, still working, as we will see, under many of the same stereotypic prejudices, amplified by the masculine culture at the Maritime College. Garrison contended that "The prevalence of women would profoundly affect the process of professionalization...The nature of library work itself ... would serve to perpetuate the low status of women in American society" (174).

Conversely, Canfield, in her 1993 thesis for her Master's Degree in Library Science, maintained that women were recruited into the library profession as an economic measure: "Because women were barred from employment in almost every other profession, they could be attracted to this one on less than equal terms. Inequality, then, was the basic condition for women's employment as librarians" (2). Schiller had made the same observation in 1974, that "libraries employed women to [their own] advantage by capitalizing on the segregation which excluded them from other fields" (*Women in Librarianship* 127). As other professions were defined as male, librarianship would become defined as female. Librarianship was beginning to evolve into an essentially "feminized" profession; women were recruited for being "softer," more willing "to serve," and having a "housekeeping instinct." Justin Winsor, historian and Superintendent of the Boston Public Library, described the value of recruiting women from colleges like Wellesley and Vassar to attend library school because "They soften our atmosphere...they are equal to our work, and for the money they cost...they are infinitely better than equivalent salaries will produce by the other sex" (in Schiller *Women in Librarianship* 127). In 1938 Ruth Savord, librarian at the Council of Foreign Relations, wrote, "We women are not wholly free from blame for this situation. For all too long, we have been satisfied to be the 'power behind the throne' as assistants to the man in charge; to take pleasure in doing the job well without any ballyhoo and without seeking or wanting any particular recognition" (342).

Hildenbrand ("Revision") and Polly Welts Kaufman both wrote critical reviews of the Garrison book. From a feminist point of view, Garrison was faulted for blaming women themselves for accepting, and thereby being responsible for, the inferior status of the library profession. By internalizing the stereotype of librarianship, women were said to have perpetuated the servile image of the profession and to have done themselves a disservice. The argument is reminiscent of Magavero's regrets at not having fought harder against ingrained prejudices at the Maritime College. Feminization would be both effect and cause of the low esteem in which librarians were viewed and would, according to Hildenbrand, result in

> overlooking or denying the centrality of women to library development, and the failure to confront the view that holds women responsible for the woes of the profession suggest a policy of containment or damage control and not the needed transformation ("A Historical

Perspective on Gender Issues in American Librarianship" 21).

Kaufman's 1983 critique of Garrison addressed the issue of agency and disputed Garrison's contention that women's passivity was one cause of their low professional status. Echoing Joan Kelly's thesis, Kaufman wrote that "Society, in fact, did *not* move steadily and ever upward toward greater tolerance" (85). Kaufman argued that librarians really did believe in the high moral imperative of delivering books and ideas to people and that they did not act impassively, as Garrison had concluded. While Kaufman's critiques are beyond the scope of this thesis, it is worthwhile noting that her argument with Garrison, supported by Schiller's seminal study which will be considered later, is that women were a majority in the profession because the salaries were low. They were, as we have seen, a good resource, a newly educated group that could be exploited at low wages because women were allowed few other opportunities. The presence of women did not cause, but was rather an effect of, low wages. Kaufman's main and most telling criticism, however, was that more detailed research was needed to determine the cause and effect of discrimination against women in the profession.

From the beginning of the professionalization of librarianship, when Melvil Dewey opened the first school to train women as librarians in 1887 at Columbia College in New York City, it was clear that women were not to be groomed for, or considered for, top positions. Although Dewey wanted to educate women, he determined that a woman should be paid less "because of the consideration which she exacts and deserves on account of her sex" (Brand 36). Dewey wrote that women *could* theoretically be as strong as men and would, under that circumstance, deserve to be paid equally, but he did not think that women would actually ever overcome this natural frailty (Dewey). In their 1974 study of the female semi-professions, Grimm and Stern felt compelled to cite a 1972 article in this footnote to their text:

> We wish to stress that sexism is not the only reason for continuation of unequal promotion policies in many occupations. Physiological factors preclude the placement and promotion of women in many segments of heavy industry and manufacturing (692).

Eighty-six years after Dewey, women were still viewed as physically inferior beings.

As early as 1929, there were articles demanding equal faculty status for librarians. In the *Peabody Journal of Education*, one of the oldest peer-reviewed journals focusing on research in education, Pearl Carson defined librarianship as a profession according to the definition in the *Oxford Dictionary*. With a combination of "knowledge and service," librarians would apply their learning and scholarship to service for library users. As professionals educated specifically in librarianship, modern librarians had progressed beyond the apprenticeship model of training, and were therefore entitled to be held in higher regard. Carson discovered, in a review of various college and university catalogs, that librarians, unlike teaching faculty, had little if any information listed about their professional qualifications or academic degrees earned (13). This was the case in Magavero's early years at the Maritime College, although by the early 1960s librarians would be listed along with faculty, with their degrees.

After World War II, when Magavero was beginning her career as a librarian, male recruitment increased. In 1938, a *Library Journal* editorial, "The Weaker Sex?" argued that because men were recruited for the best and highest paying positions in libraries, women would be relegated to lower paying jobs. The result would be a loss of talented women from the library profession. But *Library Journal* also noted that the "scarcity of qualified candidates" led to recruitment of men. The editorial posed this question: "As probably 80 to 90 percent of the members of this profession in America are composed of women, hasn't the time come to do something about it, at least, to discuss it openly among ourselves" ("The Weaker Sex?")?

The number of letters in response to the editorial, reprinted in *The Role Of Women In Librarianship: The Entry, Advancement, and Struggle for Equalization in the Profession* (Weibel, McCook and Ellsworth), shows that the answer was a resounding "yes." Most responses were from women, and all acknowledged that the problem was real. The Dean of the Library School at Emory University, Tommie Dora Barker, reviewed the history of officers and council members of the ALA. Although women were given opportunities by being nominated for various positions, they often did not get elected, and the chair of the nominating committee from 1928 to 1938 was a male. Barker wrote that "on one occasion when a suggestion of a very distinguished woman librarian for president was sent to the chairman of the Nominating Committee, he replied that sufficient time had not elapsed since the last woman was president for another to be considered, that it would be at least another year before a woman could again be considered for president!" (emphasis Barker's) (295).

Florence Curtis, another library school director, accepted the common stereotype. She thought a woman would "render more efficient service than a man [as] children's librarian." She also observed that since men had more opportunity to network and to socialize with other men in informal settings than women, they might therefore "fit in better and be more useful" in administrative positions. She concluded, however, that perhaps it did not have to be that way (Curtis).

Ruth Savord wrote in support of *Library Journal* opening the discussion. However, she did not think that women would be appropriately placed in all positions:

> By no stretch of the imagination do I think that anyone will accuse me of belonging to that detestable species known as 'feminist' or accuse me of harboring any ideas that women should be given any special consideration because they are women...Personally, it seems to me that the only library positions in this country which, in themselves, demand that the occupant shall be male are those in men's colleges and universities (342).

One male, R. M. Lightfoot, responded that men were more highly placed and better paid in all professions. He argued that because men had more opportunities in other professions, poorly paid and less qualified men could leave the profession, while poorly qualified women, with no place to go, would more likely remain in the profession. Blaming the poor image of male librarians as "sissies," he concluded that only the most devoted and talented of men would enter and stay in the library profession, and that is why so many would achieve higher positions (438). But Savord made just the opposite observation: "In a profession that has so few men proportionately the leaders naturally stand out while the truly capable woman is lost in the crowd" (343).

Hildenbrand ("A Historical Perspective on Gender Issues in American Librarianship" 19) reviewed speeches and articles from the 1940s to the early 1960s in which women were described as unfit for managerial positions and were considered to be best suited for service positions at lower pay. Both teaching and librarianship were deemed suitable for women as "motherly" and "nurturing" professions. Women's work was "to do good," to serve as a "moral compass" (Kessler-Harris). Helping the students personally was a memorable part of the job for Magavero: "So they would come and they would tell me their sad tales, and I tried to help them as much as I could, and that was another thing, that was another one of my jobs, you know but—which I enjoyed doing if I could help them" (76).

Anita Schiller's 1968 seminal work, "Characteristics of Professional Personnel in College and University Libraries," was the first specifically to examine academic libraries on a national scale and in particular to seek data by gender. This study served as an impetus for the subsequent involvement of the American Library Association in studying and addressing women's concerns in the library profession. The study was undertaken to "fill in the gap" in the lack of data about academic libraries, under the auspices of the University of Illinois' Library Research Center, and was funded by the United States Department of Health, Education, and Welfare.

As Schiller observed in 1974, although there had been studies and articles referring to women, none had ever focused on women (*Women in Librarianship*). Citing Fairchild's 1904 survey, Schiller contended that until her 1968 study, no other attempt had been made to understand the role of women in librarianship (*Women in Librarianship* 105). Mary Salome Cutler Fairchild was "one of the most influential women in librarianship" according to a note in the 1992 reprint of Fairchild's 1904 article. She taught at Columbia Library School, and followed Dewey to Albany. "Many felt that Fairchild deserved as much credit as Dewey for the influence of this [Albany] program on later library education" (S6, editorial note in reprint) . Fairchild's survey of one hundred libraries demonstrated that women "hold a large number of important positions, seldom the most important. They do not hold positions offering the highest salaries, and broadly speaking, apparently do not receive equal remuneration for the same grade of work" (S7). Fairchild thought that because there were so many women librarians, they would work for less money than men. She wrote that it was "generally conceded" that women were more apt to be gracious hosts and to "delight in self sacrifice," and that, true to stereotype, women were preferable to men as catalogers because of their "greater conscientiousness, patience and accuracy in details..." (S7).

According to Schiller, the library profession was reluctant to study or address the issue of sex discrimination for many years, and this reluctance resulted in librarians who "unconsciously, but understandably, internalized the prevailing societal view of the inherent worthiness and capability of the male and the corresponding inadequacy of the female" (*Women in Librarianship* 104). This is a fairly accurate description of the attitudes that prevailed on the Maritime College campus when Magavero began her career there. In 1973 Tarr, citing both Schiller and Auerbach, wrote that librarianship would continue to be viewed as a female profession until the profession itself raised the status of women to be equal to that of men. In 1992, Harris made the same argument in her book *Librarianship: the Erosion of a Woman's Profession*, and spoke at an ALA COSWL [Committee on the Status of Women in Librarianship] conference. She said that "Women tend to blame themselves for being unprofessional, rather than blaming external factors" ("Librarianship: Erosion or Empowerment?" 2). Magavero, although aware of the sexist situation at Maritime, still blamed herself somewhat when she spoke of her "disservice to the profession."

It was very difficult to overcome the stereotypes. In a speech to the Association of College and Research Libraries (ACRL) Annual Conference in 1989, Sarah M. Pritchard, a librarian at the Library of Congress, said,

> Women (and men) will conform to current styles and choose the course of least change because there may be little support or professional reward for anything else....The male model is still the most powerful." She continued with a statement that is an accurate assessment of Magavero's situation at the Maritime College: "Thus, making changes in one job or organization will not necessarily motivate people to change their behavior or to adopt new values if they define themselves against a broader arena, and that arena seems not to be oriented to these new behaviors." Pritchard concluded, "The frustrated attempts to implement change remind us not of the failures of feminism, but of the persistence of patriarchal thought (77).

Again, Magavero's regrets "not having fought harder" must be dismissed against the backdrop of persistent sex discrimination in profession as a whole, which was only magnified at the Maritime College.

Schiller's 1968 study, covering the 1964-65 academic year, is valuable in many ways. Two-thirds of the academic librarians discussed in this study were women, yet "When all professional and technical occupations are taken together, the ratio of women to men is almost exactly reversed" (*Characteristics* 20). There was a high (ninety-three percent) response rate which resulted in data from 2,282 full time library employees (*Characteristics* 1).

Schiller studied academic librarians by age, sex, experience, rank, and salaries, among other criteria. Until her study, there was no data on how many academic librarians held the fifth-year library degree, which Magavero had, as opposed to the Master's degree (which was not codified in accreditation standards in the library profession until 1951). By the mid-1960s, almost sixty percent of Schiller's sample held Library Science Master's degrees, while about twenty-two percent held the fifth-year Bachelor's degrees in Library Science.

Schiller discovered that not only were library salaries low in general, but also that there was a gap between what men and women earned, which could not be attributed solely to experience or education. In an article from the March 1965 *Monthly Labor Review* (Rutzick), using 1959 salary data from the 1960 census, male librarians were listed just below bus drivers, but above cabinetmakers, in salary level, which, as Schiller noted, was far below the salaries of other professional occupations. In this survey of male workers, librarians' salaries were ranked 219 out of 321 occupations selected for the comparison. Rutzick, Mobilization Coordinator of the Bureau of Labor Statistics, concluded that when women represented a high proportion in any profession, such as teaching, librarianship and nursing, salaries were lower for the entire profession (254). While women were a majority within the profession, they were a minority in academic libraries. (*Characteristics* 12)

That female faculty in colleges amounted to only about 20% of the faculty in 1962 (Parrish, cited in Schiller *Characteristics*) underscores the predominance of women in the library field. By 1970, thirty-seven percent of male librarians, but only thirteen percent of female librarians, worked in academic libraries (Irvine 10). Schiller had shown that between 1930, when males comprised nine percent of academic librarians, the percentage increased to fourteen by 1960, and to just over thirty-six percent in 1968 (*Characteristics* 45). Even Carolyn Heilbrun, a tenured professor at Columbia, felt like an outsider. Heilbrun fought and openly expressed her anger at this exclusion. She was inside the academy, yet remained an outsider until, after thirty-two years, she angrily left Columbia in 1992. Imagine how much more difficult Magavero's isolation was. Magavero was a minority within a minority at Maritime, as the only female librarian, and the only female professional at the Maritime College. Irvine cited Caplow's (Caplow and McGee) observation that "women tend to be discriminated against in the academic profession, not because they have low prestige but because they are outside the prestige system entirely" (Irvine 11-12), certainly Magavero's situation at Maritime.

Schiller's study is helpful for this thesis since a quarter of the respondents received their "first professional" or library degree before 1950, as did Magavero. Faculty rank, held by over half of the respondents, had been granted to SUNY librarians in 1968. Magavero also fit Schiller's profile of the majority of women in the study; she had majored in the humanities, as had fifty percent of respondents in the study, and like almost eleven percent of women in the study, she had majored in foreign languages and literature (*Characteristics* 37). Magavero, like the majority of female respondents, had also worked full time in non-library jobs (although most respondents had come from education) and was married. Although Schiller found that women held "a more significant share of the top positions in smaller libraries" (*Characteristics* 13), this was not the case at the Maritime College Library. Yet Magavero expressed general satisfaction with her career, a sentiment reflected in many of the comments by librarians in Schiller's study.

In 1948, Lancaster bemoaned the lack of public understanding of librarians: "Many people have the misconception that librarianship means little more than clerical duties....They look upon librarianship as a quiet, sheltered profession, and picture librarians as frustrated old ladies" (175). Even earlier, in 1923, a Carnegie Report had concluded that "Library schools are noticeably lacking in the prestige enjoyed by professional schools generally." Third on the list of "reasons for this condition" was "the preponderance of women in the faculty and student body" (Williamson 142). In a survey of academic librarians, still an understudied group in 1991, Pamela J. Cravey distinguished between the "occupational image, a euphemism for stereotype" and "occupational identity, or self-perception," and she suggested that most of the literature focused on the former rather than the latter (150-51). Like Schiller, she had a high response rate (83.6%) (154). Her data showed a poor self-image among the academic librarians surveyed, despite high job satisfaction. Another study by Detlefsen *et al*. reflected the same image: "*The word* librarian *still produces a mental image of an unmarried older…woman who is rigid and disciplined to a fault*" (Detlefsen, Olson and Frieze 36) [Authors' italics].

Along with many demographic criteria such as race and marital status, Magavero also matched many of the profiles Cravey described, such as high job satisfaction and enjoying the challenge of librarianship (154). Magavero stated that she "loved the variety" of the job, loved sleuthing, to be "asked for by name," and to "find an elusive fact"(73). The thrill of discovery was also noted by a librarian who said, "Sometimes I feel like a private eye," in an article in *Cosmopolitan*. "So much for Marian the Librarian!" the author wrote in "Shh! There Are Great Jobs in the Library," an ironically stereotypic title for an article which described various types of librarianship as career choices (Cushine).

In the Detlefsen *et al*. University of Pittsburgh library school study, the second most important reason for being a librarian was "helping people" (Detlefsen, Olson and Frieze 41). Magavero loved to advise and help the cadets, who were mostly the first in their usually blue-collar families to attend college. She "identified with them," and was often the only person they could confide in (Magavero 77). Yet by 1991, when she would officially retire, "There was little indication in the comparisons of the [1983] COSWL and [1986] Pitt studies that much had changed for women librarians" (Detlefsen, Olson and Frieze 36).

In the oral history Magavero herself subscribed, probably unconsciously, to the concept of the nurturing librarian, an empathetic and helpful person. She decided to stay at the Maritime College, even though the faculty treated her with "a mean spirit, throwing pieces of paper at her and saying 'type this.'" Magavero might have appreciated Helen Tuttle's statement that "in academic libraries, we do *not* want to eliminate men from librarianship. We simply want to teach them to take minutes, to type and to make coffee" (2596). Magavero did know that she was treated unfairly:

> They were high and mighty people. And here I am, with much more education, and I was hired as a clerk. Now I questioned that of the librarian at the time, you know, I thought, 'Why should I be in the clerical line?' He said, 'Well, there's nothing I could do, you know this is the way it is,' and you know I accepted (63).

Kelly described "the need to feel superior, and the displaced sexual feelings, [that] made up a good part of the psychology of educated men" (81). Magavero was isolated, and lacked the models to help her understand that her plight was not unique, nor within her purview to change.

This attitude towards, and perception of, librarians was not so unusual. In his 1923 study of library education, C. C. Williamson found that the public considered library work to be "wholly clerical," and that the library schools were not doing enough to counter this perception (Williamson). In Schiller's 1968 study, she found this perception still to be a problem. Although professionals are differentiated from clerical workers by advanced educational requirements, Schiller cited the 1966-67 *Occupational Outlook Handbook*'s caption on a photo of a librarian as "someone who checks out books, a specifically clerical job in libraries, requiring no advanced degrees or training" (*Characteristics* 61). Magavero decided to "just ignore them," and to do her work well. She describes how she came to love the job, even though she did not "have a single friend on the [all-male] faculty" (67).

In 1972, Auerbach described more fully the position of women in academic libraries. Using Carol Andreas's "caste" analogy, Auerbach portrayed a "harem" atmosphere in the library world, in which men led and women were subordinate, much as in social work, teaching, and nursing (2). In a vicious circle, the "self-perpetuating" stereotypic expectations undermine advancement, which in turn is halted by discrimination based on the lack of women in higher (usually administrative) positions. Citing unpublished reports, Auerbach discussed the imbalance of women to men in top positions at University of Wisconsin Memorial Library. She also speculated that women did not advance because of the entrenched male culture and resulting seniority in academia, an accurate characterization of the situation at the Maritime College. Auerbach's own research led her to conclude that there was in fact more discrimination against women in academic than in public libraries and that this discrimination was due to gender bias (4-6).

When the ALA survey was completed in 1970-71, it was the first time that the study of salaries had been distinguished by gender. Brugh and Beede suggested that although 1970 was a beginning for the study of salary differentials, no one was willing to look at the data and extrapolate sex discrimination, arguing that other factors such as education, mobility and experience needed to be considered. In other words, the salary gap was acknowledged, but the reasons for it were not recognized. But the Special Library Association (SLA) surveyed salaries by gender in 1970 and found "evidence of a real male-oriented bias in salaries of all categories" (SLA 348). Moreover, the study concluded that the twenty-five percent gap in salary was due not to differences in education or status, but only to the gender difference (Brugh and Beede 947). Cooper came to the same conclusion in his review of research on sex and salary in 1976 (Cooper 329), as did Dowell in 1988 (97).

Beginning in 1972, Carlyle J. Frarey and Carol L. Learmont produced annual salary surveys for *Library Journal* which tabulated salaries by gender: "The lowest salary reported for a man was higher than the lowest for a woman in each type [of library]" (2159). However, they were only willing to say that their data "reinforce[s] what we have long known: that whether or not there is any real discrimination intended or practiced, men, in general, fare better in their beginning salaries than do women" (1767). In 1972, and again in 1976, salary surveys of public librarians in *Library Journal* showed clear evidence of sex discrimination, both in salary and promotion (Carpenter).

In 1995, Kelley A. Lawton prepared a study of the career of a woman librarian at the University of North Carolina's School of Library Science (Lawton). Although SUNY Maritime and University of North Carolina are very different in many ways, from the compositions of student body to their respective missions, there are similarities between the careers of Susan Grey Akers and Filomena Magavero. Akers, reflecting on her career, described the University of North Carolina as a "man's university for so long" (Lawton 17), as were most coeducational universities in the United States. Akers was Dean of the Library School at North Carolina from 1932 to 1954. Thus the end of her career overlapped with the beginning of Magavero's. Akers attended library school because, like Magavero, she disliked teaching. Akers was "tolerated but not completely accepted, and the traditional ideas of women's place in the world still had a foothold" (Lawton 17). Magavero was neither welcomed nor completely tolerated at Maritime. During her first two years at Maritime, she was not even allowed to use a bathroom near the library in which to wash her hands. She was the butt of jokes, just as Maude Malone had been at the 1919 ALA convention when she tried to get an equal pay resolution passed.

While women made up twenty percent of all librarians in 1876, by 1910, the United States census reported that seventy-nine percent were women. In 1950, when Magavero began her career at New York Maritime, the percentage of women in the profession had increased to ninety and had dropped only to eighty percent by 1970 (Schiller *Women in Librarianship* 125). Schiller's 1970 article, "The Disadvantaged Majority; Women Employed in Libraries," laid the groundwork for the formation of the Committee on the Status of Women in Librarianship (COSWL). Ultimately, the effects of society's view of women were the same when discriminating against women in the library profession, whether they were conscious or unconscious policies and actions. The lack of data and studies hampered arguments of discriminatory practices in the field. In Schiller's work, she cited studies which compared sex-typing in other professions and related them to librarianship, reaffirming that sex roles in the greater society are reflected in work role assignments in libraries. Schiller argued that sexism in the library profession was "explicit" and overt and had its roots in the "complex interaction of the larger society's male/female role prescriptions" (*Women in Librarianship* 107). Auerbach concurred: "More and more the powerful effects of role expectations are being recognized" (6).

All salary surveys and studies in the 1950s established that women earned less than men, in a profession where salaries were low to begin with. Although various salary surveys were conducted in the period 1960 to 1972, according to Schiller, they each focused on a particular segment of the library profession (academic, public, law libraries, for example), but no surveys based on gender and salary were conducted on the profession as a whole. Oddly enough, as experience increased, the salary differential grew (Schiller *Women in Librarianship* 109). During this period, female librarians earned on average seventy-five percent of what male librarians earned. In academic libraries, which Schiller surveyed for 1966-1967, she found that the average women's salary was eighty-three percent of that of men. The differential ranged from ninety-two percent for women in academic libraries with less that five years experience to seventy percent for men and women with twenty or more years of experience. The differential increase with experience is a reflection of the lower status of the jobs that women obtained.

In 1965, a *Library Journal* editorial declared an unwillingness to be "brave—or foolish—enough to take sides" or address the issue of discrimination against women in the profession (Moon). The University of California at Berkeley performed its own study in 1971, in which it found more promotions, and therefore higher salaries, for male librarians. Thus, Maritime College, even with its particular male culture, was not so different in its library staffing than the academic library world at large. In Schiller's 1968 survey, she found that academic libraries had the smallest percentage of females, sixty-two percent compared to ninety-four percent in school libraries.

The annual salary surveys published in *Library Journal* did not include data by sex until 1972. This came about as a result of a request by the Social Responsibilities Round Table Task Force on Women (SRRT), which was formed at ALA in Detroit in 1970. Indeed, surveying library literature in 2006, I discovered that out of 116 articles on salaries in *Library Journal* from 1976 through 2006, only four specifically focused on academic libraries. Additionally, the Association of Research Libraries' (ARL) annual salary studies did not analyze the results by gender until 1977 (Schuman and Weibel 325). Thus, although later research began to tease out statistics by gender, it has been difficult to locate data specifically related to librarians in academia.

Feminists in the ALA succeeded in getting the organization to cease listing jobs by sex in the early 1970s. Before that date, jobs were listed with outright gender preference, such as "Head, Undergraduate Library. Major University desires innovative young man" (Cassell 25). In 1964, an article in *Esquire* declared "Most of the top jobs in the profession want male librarians to fill them, as the running of library systems in most large urban areas of the nation is truly big business" ("Young Man, Be a Librarian"). Raising the consciousness of the profession, to use the terminology and strategy of Second Wave Feminism, became the mission of the SRRT Task Force on the Status of Women in Librarianship. In 1970, the Task Force met in Detroit and passed a resolution introduced by Anita Schiller: "Therefore, be it resolved that the American Library Association take steps to equalize salaries and opportunities for employment and promotions" (*SRRT Task Force on the Status of Women in Librarianship Newsletter*, cited in Cassell 22). Although the fact of discrimination and second class treatment of women in the profession was a given, acceptance of this lower status was built on lack of data. It took studies of the late 1970s and 1980s to reveal that women were as mobile, experienced, and educated as men (criteria used in the assumption that women should be excluded) and that they therefore were qualified for, and should be employed in, higher positions.

The SRRT began to publish a newsletter in order to publish statistics. In a 1970 salary survey, it was reported that women earned only seventy-five percent of what men earned: "only four of the seventy-four largest college and university libraries had women directors; 12 percent of women were chief librarians, but 22 percent of male librarians had achieved that status." In a self-study at the University of California at Berkeley in 1972, it was revealed that more women were hired in lower ranks than men and that "a woman must have at least twice the amount of experience as a man to be hired at a comparable level." Purdue University discovered a similar pattern of discrimination against women, noting that women needed much more experience in order to achieve the same levels of rank and salary as men (Cassell 25, citing the ALA SRRT Newsletters 1970-1972).

In 1973, Susan Tarr proposed actions to counter the stereotypic arguments against equality for women in salary and promotion. Debunking the arguments that women worked "just for pin money" and that women were not as interested as men in promotions, Tarr wrote that "this low ranking is based primarily on *subjective* rather than objective criteria" (emphasis hers) (24). These subjective criteria included the preference by women, as well as men, for male leaders "because of a conditioning to accept men as the 'appropriate' embodiment of domination and superiority" (31).

Jean Martin's study, included in Heim's 1983 anthology, compared the salaries and positions in academic libraries based on gender, and her conclusions bore out previous assertions of female predominance but male superiority in wage and higher level positions obtained (Martin). Even with increased feminist consciousness, the decade preceding this article had still not produced data specifically addressing why women were not proportionally represented in higher or management positions in libraries. As Schiller had discovered, compared to public libraries, where women held thirty-nine percent of the top positions, in academic libraries it was only eight percent. Martin examined both the ACRL 1975-1976 survey and Schiller's studies and realized there was a need to see if any variable outside of gender could explain the discrepancies between men's and women's salary levels and an upward path in their academic careers. Stereotypes and perception, both internal and external, worked against women according to the studies from the mid-1970s that Martin cited.

Women's efforts at being recognized were practically laughed out of the ALA. In 1919, Maude Malone demanded that a resolution be passed for "equal pay and opportunity for women." It was defeated 121 to 1. Malone is said to have abstained from voting, and the one pro vote remains anonymous (Schuman and Weibel). As late as 1970, at the ALA convention in Detroit, Betty Wilson, having been denied entry into a bar at the convention, tried to get a resolution passed so that the ALA would not hold its meetings in venues that discriminated against women: "Amid jokes about integrated bathrooms and much laughter, Membership defeats the resolution" (Schuman and Weibel 322).

The ALA's feeble involvement in addressing women's issues did not begin to change until 1969. By 1974, the SRRT formed a Task Force on the Status of Women, and so many committees and discussion groups had been organized that it was "possible to attend a feminist conference within a conference" at ALA conventions (Schuman and Weibel 323). ALA even endorsed the Equal Rights Amendment (ERA) at the 1974 convention in New York City. But the endorsement became a moot point when the amendment's ratification stalled after only thirty-five of the necessary thirty-eight states ratified it. And while the ALA passed a resolution to join the ERA boycott against holding meetings in states that had not ratified the ERA, commitment to that resolution was not strong, and the ALA met in Chicago in 1980 even though Illinois had not ratified the amendment. ALA did, however, continue to fund efforts to pass the ERA and to uphold the boycott (Bundy and Stielow 25-26).

The Committee on the Status of Women in Librarianship (COSWL) was established in the ALA in 1976, thirty years after Magavero graduated from library school. Ruth Canfield's 1993 Master's Thesis, *The ALA Committee on the Status of Women in Librarianship: an Examination of Its History and Impact*, is a detailed and comprehensive study of COSWL, exploring its mission, goals, and accomplishments. Her thesis was based on documentation provided by COSWL members, as well as questionnaires sent to some of those members. According to Canfield, lobbying for such a committee began with the publication of Schiller's "Disadvantaged Majority." (Canfield). Pay equity was one of COSWL's goals, as was equal status. Overall, the purpose of COSWL was to research and analyze data about women in the profession and in the ALA itself. Ten years after the formation of COSWL, Barbara Ivy observed that "remedy[ing] the inequities involving the status of women in the professional organization of libraries...is not the same as changing the status of women in librarianship" (Ivy 42). But COSWL did publish a very important bibliography in 1984, *On Account of Sex: An Annotated Bibliography of the Status of Women in Librarianship, 1977-1981* (Heim and Phenix), followed by a second volume covering the years 1982 to 1986 (Phenix, Goetsch and Watstein). These invaluable bibliographies would greatly enhance the ability to research women in the library profession.

At the same time librarians were examining and revising subject headings using non-sexist terms and expanding access to women's history, issues and resource collections. For example, the Library of Congress *Subject Headings* used the terms,

> 'Women *as* authors,' not 'Women authors'; 'Women *as* physicians,' not 'Women physicians'; 'Women *as* librarians,' not Women librarians,' etc. (Yet when we come to 'Women as criminals,' we are advised to refer to the heading 'Delinquent women.') While it is delightful to note the cross reference 'Women, see also Charm,'...it is clear that this terminology...in not in keeping with present conditions. (Schiller "Disadvantaged Majority" 346)

COSWL members also contributed "Women in Librarianship" to *The ALA Yearbook*, which was published annually from 1976 until 1990. (In 1984, the title was changed to the *ALA Yearbook of Library and Information Services*.) For all the work that COSWL accomplished, it was just the beginning of the quest for equality and an end to discrimination. Magavero had been a librarian for thirty years before any of this occurred.

THE MARITIME COLLEGES

The five state maritime schools instruct men (and since the mid-1970s women) in seamanship to qualify as officers in the United States Merchant Marine. At different points in time, the various state schools added academic requirements and were authorized to grant Bachelor's degrees. But their core mission, regimental in nature, is training a corps of seafarers.

The State University of New York (SUNY) Maritime College began as the Nautical School *St. Mary's* to train young men to serve on merchant, as opposed to military, ships. In 1874, the Congress of the United States approved the loan of the sloop of war *St. Mary's* to the Board of Education of the City of New York for use as a schoolship. By living on the ship, boys could now receive instruction in navigation, naval architecture, seamanship, and marine engineering. It was the only such nautical school in the country. The boys lived on the ship, moored in the East River at 23rd Street, and wore uniforms for work and dress. The dress uniforms, with cap and gold braid, were military in appearance; the discipline and organization of the school were also military in style. The curriculum included basic courses in reading, writing, Bible, geography, arithmetic, spelling and grammar, in addition to the nautical training (Rideing). There was a training cruise every year, usually to some European ports. The archives at the Maritime College hold the logs of the training cruises, and provide a marvelous window into the life on board the vessels. The Maritime College library also owns a copy of a movie shot in 1905, showing some exercises on the *St. Mary's* (*Drills and Exercises, Schoolship "St. Mary's"*). At the end of two years (usually), the student was awarded a certificate after passing the annual examination.

After some changes in curriculum and organization, the school joined the State University of New York (SUNY) in 1948, as one of the original colleges to become part of the SUNY system. The name was changed to the New York State Maritime College. It was fully accredited as a four-year college by the Middle States Association of Colleges and Secondary Schools in 1952. (For a detailed history of the college through its 1974 Centennial, see Norman Brouwer's 1977 thesis.)

The students, called cadets, continue to wear military-style uniforms, and the regimental corps, for those enrolled in the license programs, is still considered the primary mission of the college. The first woman to graduate from SUNY Maritime, Marjorie Murtaugh, had transferred to the school in 1972. She graduated with a degree in Naval Architecture in 1974, twenty-six years after Magavero had begun working there. Murtaugh was initially rejected by the school, but the American Civil Liberties Union (ACLU) threatened a lawsuit, and the school relented. Murtaugh did not participate in the license program and was thus a day student ("Maritime College Accepts 1st Woman"). The first woman to enroll in the regimental license program graduated in 1978.

The Stephen B. Luce Library is named after Rear Admiral Stephen Bleecker Luce (1827–1917), who wrote the definitive Text-Book of Seamanship: *The Equipping and Handling of Vessels Under Sail or Steam, For the Use of The United States Naval Academy* (1898). It was Captain Luce who transferred the *St. Mary's* to the Nautical School in 1874. According to the New York State Maritime College catalog circa 1946 (the volume is undated), the library, located in the southeast section of the Fort, held about 6,000 volumes and was just beginning to develop its collection. The fort itself is a pentagonal granite edifice, constructed in 1833 and completed in 1856. In September 1948, the school adopted a four-year curriculum. At the same time, by granting Bachelor of Science degrees, the college had to agree to appoint department heads with academic degrees as well as merchant marine licenses.

By 1949, the library held 12,000 volumes and was growing. In December 1965, the library was finally relocated to a large new space. The square footage was increased to accommodate up to 80,000 volumes, compared to the 10,000-volume capacity of the old space. By this time, 45,000 volumes were in the collection, including 7,000 that were moved from storage to the open stacks. The dedication took place on the 100th anniversary of the transfer of the *St. Mary's*, December 10, 1974 (Brouwer 117), when the library was renamed in honor of Admiral Luce.

When Filomena Magavero began her career at SUNY Maritime College in 1949, she was entering a male bastion that would not hire another female faculty member until 1965, when Libby S. Hummer appeared in the catalog as an "Interne Instructor" in the Humanities Department. Hummer was gone, however, by the next year. In 1971 Janet Pomeranz was hired to teach mathematics in the Science Department; the first full-time female Assistant Professor. She was followed by Karen Markoe in 1974, in the Humanities Department. Magavero was, therefore, the only professional (i.e., non-secretarial and non-janitorial) female on campus for close to thirty years.

The male culture at the Maritime was insufferable. Women were traditionally thought of as bad luck on board ships and were not welcomed on campus. It was not, in short, a place where she had any chance, hope, or even idea of advancement to higher positions, although other maritime schools in the United States did have female directors by the 1980s.

While various studies of women in academic libraries are critical for understanding women's history in librarianship, it is difficult to apply some of the data to Magavro's situation at the Maritime College. According to Schiller, only six percent of the libraries surveyed were in the "Other Professional School" category, which is most likely where Maritime would be categorized, since it was considered a "Specialized" college within the SUNY system. It would be more appropriate to compare Magavero's career to those of librarians at the four other state maritime colleges, and also to the Federal Merchant Marine Academy, since they all operated within the same all-male culture and regimented structure.

In surveying the *American Library Directory* ("American Library Directory; a Classified List of Libraries in the United States and Canada, with Personnel and Statistical Data"), comparative data is difficult to obtain because not all of the maritime libraries report their statistics every year. Additionally, many librarians are listed by initials and not first names, making it difficult to ascertain gender.

In the 1954 ALA Directory, the Luce Library was found under State University of New York, Maritime College Library. Filomena I. Magavero was listed in Technical Processes, along with the two male librarians, Terence J. Hoverter, Librarian (i.e., director) and Maurice Rahilly, Readers' Services (i.e., reference). That same year, Maine's was the only other Maritime institution listed, whose librarian is listed as LCDR. H.E. Small. Its library, with 2000 volumes, was considerably smaller than New York's, which held 25,000 volumes.

In 1960, New York listed only Magavero and Hoverter on staff. The United States Merchant Marine Academy

(USMMA) at King's Point was listed for the first time. The librarian and associate librarian were both men with ranks of Lieutenant Commander, but neither Mrs. Jeanne Schwartz, in Technical Processes, nor Leona Haviland, Interlibrary loan and Reference librarian, had regimental ranks. At 35,000 volumes, the U.S. Merchant Marine Academy was comparable to the Luce Library's 33,000 volumes. Texas Maritime's library held only 1000 volumes. The director, however, was a woman, which reflects the findings in several surveys that women rose to high administrative positions mainly in smaller libraries. The only other librarian on the staff, a cataloger, was male. Massachusetts Maritime Academy, is the closest in size and history to New York Maritime. Since October 2005, there has been a female director of the Captain Charles H. Hurley Library.

Maine Maritime Academy is smaller than either Mass or SUNY Maritime. Founded in 1941, the library was established shortly thereafter, although there was no full-time professional librarian until 1969. By 1990, through reorganization, the librarians lost their faculty status. Although the first woman was not hired until about 1972, in 1983 Marjorie Harrison became the library director and the first female department chair at Maine Maritime. In 1997, she was succeeded by another woman, Wendy Knickerbocker, who left in 2002.

California Maritime was established in 1929, but did not formally have a library until 1959, when the first professional librarian was hired. Darcus Thomas was the first female librarian, hired in 1981. Texas Maritime was established in 1961, as part of the Texas A & M system. It is smaller than either Massachusetts or SUNY. Peggy Leadaman was the Jack K. Williams Library director in 1976. She was replaced by the current director, Natalie

Wiest, in 1982. Ironically, Texas did not hire a male librarian until about 1985.

The United States Merchant Marine Academy is across the Long Island Sound from Ft. Schuyler. In 1973, the Maritime Administration (MARAD), which oversaw maritime education in the United States, reversed the longstanding exclusion of women from entering merchant marine license programs, and King's Point admitted its first female student (U.S. Merchant Marine Academy). Beth Fuseler Avery was the director at King's Point's Schuyler Otis Bland Library from 1981 to 1983. As Director, she held the rank of Commander and was the only librarian to hold any rank.

So, although women were not accepted as students at the maritime academies until the mid-1970s, Texas, Maine, and King's Point all had women in top library management long before SUNY or Massachusetts. And although all those academies have shorter histories, they were still all founded before the Second Wave made inroads into academia, and they still had male-only student bodies when they had women directors. Perhaps Texas, Maine and King's Point were more able to accept women as library directors because their traditions were not so entrenched; because they did not have hundred year-old practices from the nineteenth century, they were more able to accept women as library directors.

MRS. MAGAVERO

Filomena Martemucci was born on October 20, 1922, in Bronx, New York, the oldest of three girls. Her mother was a homemaker, and her father owned a shoe repair shop. After graduating from Evander Childs High School in 1939, she attended Hunter College, where she majored in Romance languages and graduated in 1943. Proficient in French and Italian, she had planned to teach but became "disenchanted" with teaching after the training period during her last year at Hunter. The United States was involved in World War II, and, wanting to contribute to the war effort, she applied for a job with the Office of Censorship. Because of her language skills, she was hired to read letters intercepted from enemy countries. She was part of the generation of women who trained and worked during the war, yet were not given much opportunity when the men returned from the war. In 1938, Savord, librarian at the Council of Foreign Relations, made the following observation about women after the First World War: "We do have a large 'war generation' of women who have been acquiring experience over a period of almost twenty years," she wrote in her letter, bemoaning the "apparent discrimination against [women's] advancement" (342).

Magavero worked at the Office of Censorship until the war ended in 1945. That September, she enrolled in Columbia University's Library School and received her Bachelor of Science degree in Library Science in June 1946. Having loved working in libraries during both high school and at Hunter College, she felt that this would be her calling. In June 1951, she married Joseph Magavero, a lawyer.

Her first job, as Assistant Cataloger, was at the United States Merchant Marine Academy in King's Point, New York. The woman who was head of cataloging had been in the Navy, and as Magavero said, she had expertise and experience with the military structure of the school and thereby also had the respect of her colleagues on the faculty; she was comfortable with and accepted by the King's Point faculty. However, Magavero's pay was quite low, as hers was only an entry- level job. After about a year and a half, she was offered the job as Head of Cataloging at Hunter College. She accepted, with the encouragement of her boss, because the salary offered, $1800 per year, was, in Magavero's own words, "monumentally high."

But she had been happy at King's Point and did not like the job at Hunter. She then met Terry Hoverter, the library director at the New York State Nautical School, which is what the Fort Schuyler campus was called at that time. She made the long trek from her home in the northwest Bronx to Fort Schuyler, in the Throg's Neck section in the extreme southeast part of the Bronx. To this day, transportation to the peninsula on which the Fort is located is difficult. Magavero arrived after a snow storm, and walked about a mile from the bus to the library. (Ironically, in 1994, I was also interviewed in the aftermath of a huge snowstorm, but I *drove* to the campus and *drove* by the huge mounds of fresh snow.) And although she thought to herself that she could not take the job because of the lack of transportation, she did accept the offer of employment, and commuted to Fort Schuyler for the next fifty-four years. Despite a long commute on public transportation (she never learned to drive), she was almost always the first to arrive (at 7:30 AM) and often the last to leave.

When Magavero was hired at the Maritime College, she had not only her Bachelor's degree from Hunter College, she also had a Bachelor of Science degree from Columbia University. Yet she was hired on a clerical line, and worked at this level for thirteen years, beginning on March 1, 1949. Her claim that "one-third of the faculty at the time had studies only at schoolship level" and "had only professional but not academic credentials" (63) is not completely borne out by a review of faculty listed in the college catalog during the 1950s. It was not true of the engineering department, one of the two core programs (those that led to the merchant marine licenses) at the college. But the faculty in the Marine transportation department (deck, as opposed to engine oriented studies) did not have more than Bachelor's degrees or professional certifications or licenses.

In the 1950 Maritime College Yearbook, *Eight Bells* ("Eight Bells : Yearbook of the New York State Maritime Academy, Fort Schuyler, New York"), Magavero is flanked by two men in uniform, although no one is named; the caption, as with other departments, simply reads "Library Staff."

LIBRARY STAFF

MRS. MAGAVERO 51

The next picture, from the 1952 yearbook, shows Mrs. Magavero in a dress, flanked by Lt. Cdr. O'Hara and Cdr. Hoverter, both in uniform.

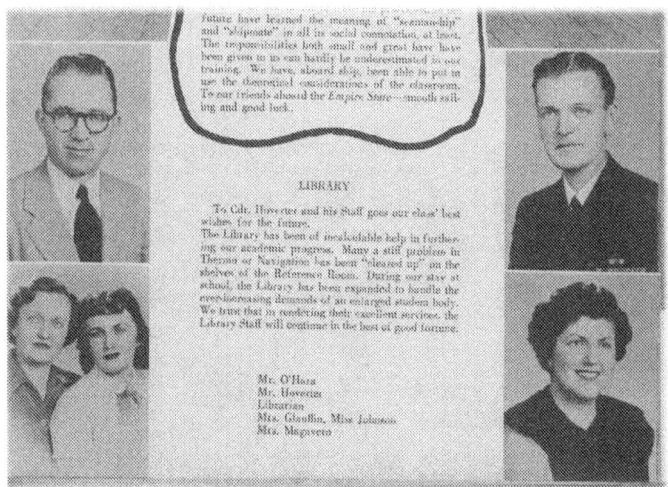

In the 1953 yearbook, only Hoverter, with the rank of Commander, was identified as a librarian. Mr. O'Hara and Mrs. Magavero were listed along with the clerical staff, with no captions to distinguish between professional and clerical staff.

MRS. MAGAVERO

In the 1954 Yearbook, the two men are identified as librarians, but Mrs. Magavero has no title. She is indistinguishable from the female clerical staff.

Not until the 1956 yearbook was Magavero identified as Assistant Librarian, although she was still working in a clerical line.

She was the only female librarian until the mid-1960s, when another woman, Gail Hitt, was hired in the acquisitions department of the library. During Magavero's tenure at the library there were only three directors. Terence Hoverter was succeeded in 1961 by Dr. Joseph N. (Nat) Whitten, who was in turn succeeded by Richard H. Corson, who was promoted to Librarian in 1970. There was not a female director until 2001.

While nearby City University of New York (CUNY) librarians were granted faculty status in 1965, SUNY librarians did not receive academic rank until 1968, after a campaign led by Dr. Whitten begun in 1966 (DeVinney). This rank entitled them to tenure, peer review and sabbaticals, but not academic year appointment (which SUNY librarians still do not have in 2006) or salary or rank parity with faculty. The following year, in January 1969, SUNY librarians formed the SUNY Librarians Association (SUNYLA) to lobby for full faculty status. The issue for librarians was to be able to work an academic calendar year, like teaching faculty, without taking a loss in pay because they no longer would be working on a twelve-month calendar. Although librarian ranks were agreed to by the Chancellor of the University and the Department of Budget for the state of New York in 1971, they were not implemented until 1976. It was not until 1985 that librarians received the same salary scale as professional faculty in the union (United University Professionals, or UUP) contract for 1985-1988.

Shortly after Magavero was hired as a cataloger, one of the "behind the scenes" places that were deemed most appropriate for women, a male was hired as a reference librarian, in a librarian, not clerical, rank. Describing sex typing in occupations, Carol Andreas wrote: "The concept of *caste* conveys how social roles are determined by birth rather than by achievement. In a society not conditioned by *caste*, work roles would be assigned or chosen according to individual aptitudes" (Andreas 48) . Fred O'Hara was made an officer in the regiment of the Maritime College, and was paid more than Magavero. He was a "member of the club," and Hoverter told Magavero there was nothing he could do about her lower rank, or lower salary.

When a reference position became available, Magavero asked to be transferred. The library director

> went around canvassing all the department chairs, 'What would you think if we put Fil Magavero at the reference desk [usually the first and most public face of the library].' I mean shouldn't she be behind the scenes as a cataloger for the rest of her life? You know, that kind of thing, that kind of stupidity. You know when I think of it now, nobody else would have taken it as long as I did, but I was too chicken (Magavero 64).

This was not an atypical situation, as we have seen in Martin's study of positions in academic libraries: "In academic environments, where males predominate on faculties and in administrative positions (an understatement regarding the Maritime College), it is felt by many that male library managers fit in better, since they would be more readily accepted as leaders than females" (Martin 250). Magavero understood her place as a woman, and that they thought she should stay behind the scenes [as a cataloger] for the rest of her life.

Eventually, the practice of giving rank (with the requisite uniforms) to librarians and faculty faded, except when they were teaching on the training ship. However, the women librarians on the cruise were not assigned rank, and women who were hired as Ship's Librarians did not have an easy time. Usually hired just for the two-month long cruise, they were not only outsiders as women, but also were not part of the Maritime College male faculty that taught on the training ship. When asked if she had ever wanted to work as Ship's Librarian, Magavero just laughed replied that she was almost sixty by the time they allowed women on the ship.

Magavero worked at a place, and in a time, which limited her opportunities for advancement and promotion. Not only was the male culture at the Maritime College hostile and even intimidating; the library profession itself actually discouraged women from seeking higher administrative and directorial positions. The "feminization" of the profession, much like that of social work and teaching, other traditionally service (read nurturing or caring) professions, kept wages low and career paths did not head far up the ladder.

The American Library Association did not address the issues of discrimination against women, whether in status, salary, or other equity problems until 1976, by which time Magavero had been a librarian for almost thirty years. The Committee on the Status of Women in Librarianship (COSWL) first published a *Directory of Library and Information Profession Women's Groups* in 1980 and produced several editions annually after that. Magavero was not only isolated as the only woman at Maritime, and by lack of travel opportunities, but also because there had never been such a directory before 1980. Her isolation was physical, both because of the location of Fort Schuyler and her exclusion by the male faculty. It was also psychological and emotional, because of a lack of support systems providing contact with other women professionals. There simply was no mechanism for such support in the 1950s and 1960s.

CONCLUSION

Lest we think that library stereotypes have disappeared, an article in the *New York Times* on March 14, 2006, began this way: "The bibliothèques of Paris don't suffer from the dowdy image problem that afflicts libraries in the United States" (Wooward). In *Library Journal* on February 1, 2006, a student graduating from UCLA's Department of Information Studies found it necessary to develop a blog and a set of library trading cards to "bring librarians into the spotlight [in order to] change the stereotypes" ("Librarians Get Their Cards" 223).

The ARL Salary Survey for 2003-2004 found that women still earn less than men: "The gender gap in ARL university salaries still exists, even though ARL libraries have remained approximately 65% female since 1980-81…As in past years, differentials in experience do not explain this phenomenon; there are several categories in which women average more experience but lower salaries"(Young 8). The SLA Salary Survey for 2003 found that even though in 1999 SLA had declared that "gender equity" had been achieved, in 2003 there was again a gap, albeit a small one, and men again earned more than women (Latham 16).

As we have seen, although there is a great deal of history of women in libraries, there is a dearth of readily discoverable information about individual women in the profession. Much of the history of women in libraries is still hidden in archives and repositories. A search of WorldCat, an international database of library holdings, reveals the paucity of catalogued and available information. One must drill deep into brief descriptions of archival materials to ascertain what *might* be extensive or merely peripheral biographical information on women librarians in the nineteen oral histories about women in libraries. Most published library history is not about the women who worked in the profession. A search on "women academic librarians" for archival materials yields thirteen results, but it is not clear from any of the descriptions just how much real biographical information about women as librarians in academia might be in these collections. It would require an actual physical examination of these manuscript collections to uncover more history of women in academic libraries. Most of these papers are about women who were librarians in the 19th and very early 20th centuries.

A subject search in WorldCat.org on "Women librarians --United States--Biography" yields twenty-one titles, ten of which are books. Of these books, two are for a juvenile audience, and both are about the same woman, Beverly Cleary, while one title is fiction. Of the seven other titles, only four are actual biographies.

There are twenty-two unique titles that result from searching "Women librarians--United States--Interviews." Fortunately, more research is being done in this area, as many of these interviews were conducted in the 1980's and 1990's. In 1980, Kathryn Renfro Lundy published a collection of interviews entitled *Women View Librarianship: Nine Perspectives* for the ALA, which also published Katherine de la Peña McCook's *Women of color in librarianship : an oral history* in 1998 as a direct result of COSWL's work.

Searching in WorldCat for biographies of women librarians in the United States, excluding fiction and juvenile titles, yields a mere six hits, which includes four books, one archival collection, and one briefly described archival collection that *may* include some relevant material. The librarians written about worked mostly in the earlier part of the 20th century. Broadening the search to "librarians" yields 179 books and fourteen archival records, five of which are about women: three academic librarians, one special librarian, and one a public librarian. Dates are inexact, as is the cataloging, since these records should ideally be added to the subject of women in libraries. It would be worth examining these archival collections to further explore the history of women in academic libraries. Other books, such as *The Dismissal of Miss Ruth Brown*, about an African-American woman who was a librarian in Oklahoma, are scattered among different subject headings which do not reflect their biographical content, and don't appear in the biography subject area.

Suzanne Hildenbrand's essay "Library lives in multidimensional reality" in *Women of color in librarianship : an oral history* discusses women's history in libraries in terms of Gerda Lerner's historiography. Lerner emphasized the importance of placing individual lives in multiple contexts, so that not only gender, but also race, class, and ethnicity would be considered. It is important to consider the overlap between these contexts to achieve a fuller integration of women into library history, instead of "melting" women librarians into library history, in which case their stories are subverted by that of men in the profession. Women were denied employment or promotion not only because of gender, but in some cases because of marital status, race, or ethnicity. Magavero's story clearly resides in the gender category.

Theresa Tobin's 1998 preface to *Women of color in librarianship* quotes from the ALA handbook about the goals the ALA set for COSWL to disseminate and coordinate information on the status of women in librarianship. Clearly, there is a lot of hard work yet to be done to mine this data and create a robust history of the women who worked in libraries. As Schiller, Detlefsen, Cravey, Cooper and Dowell had all discovered in their research in the 1960s through the 1990s, women continue to be a "disadvantaged majority." Neither two waves of feminism, nor consciousness-raising, nor the law, have leveled the playing field yet. We may never know with any certainty which came first, low status or low salaries. If we cannot determine where the cycle began, it is still imperative to break the cycle with more research and more opportunity. The library world has come a long way since 1949, but still has a long way to go.

I hope that more research will be done on this important subject, and I am glad to have had the opportunity to record Filomena Magavero's unique career as a contribution to the dissemination of women's history.

AFTERWORD

In June, 2007, SUNYLA held its 39th Annual Conference at the Maritime College, where the Luce library staff honored Mrs. Magavero and presented her with a plaque in appreciation for her lifetime achievement at the Luce Library.

In Honor of Filomena I. Magavero

For her numerous achievements:

The 1st female librarian at the former New York Maritime Academy, now known as SUNY Maritime College.

Contributing 54 years of employment and voluntary service to the library profession.

Participating as an inaugural SUNYLA member and delegate.

Mrs. Magavero has played an integral role in the history of SUNYLA and the library profession within the State University System. Since 1949 she has served as the consummate professional and a shining example of librarianship.

We are forever grateful.

Presented at the
State University of New York Librarians Association
(SUNYLA)
39th Annual Conference
On June 15, 2007

Stephen B. Luce Library,
State University of New York, Maritime College

TRANSCRIPT OF ORAL HISTORY

Interview with Filomena I. Magavero

Jane: My name is Jane Brodsky Fitzpatrick. I'm 57 years old. Today is November 3rd, 2005, and we are at Grand Central Terminal in New York City, and I was a co-worker with Filomena for about ten years.

Fil: And my name is Filomena Magavero. I'm 83 years old. Today is November 3rd, 2005, and I am at Grand Central Terminal with Jane Fitzpatrick who was my co-worker for ten years.

Jane: Fil, librarianship, as we know, is historically a profession dominated by women. Can you tell me when you decided to go to graduate school and particularly to library school?

Fil: Okay, I went to Columbia after World War II. I had always worked in libraries, my high school library, and my college library. But when I went to Hunter to get my Bachelor's Degree, I thought I wanted to be a teacher. When I did teacher training in my last year at Hunter, I was disenchanted. I graduated from Hunter in 1943—World War II—I graduated in January of '43, so World War II had already been going for over a year, and I thought at that time, "I really don't want to go into teaching, I want to do something in the war effort like everybody else was doing at that time," so I looked for a job that would make me happy doing something other than teaching. And one of my teachers recommended that I try doing some work with translating, because my major in college was Romance Languages, and I was quite proficient in Italian and French, which I was hoping to teach. But I never got there. So I looked for something that would do that for me, and I found out that The Office of Censorship was looking for translators. What they were doing, they were looking to intercept mail coming out of enemy countries at the time, and reviewing the mail to see whether they could obtain any intelligence in those countries before our troops invaded, or whatever.

So I applied for the job, and it took a little while before the job came through, and in the meantime I looked for my great love [laughs]—I looked for a job at The New York Public Library until I was called by The Office of Censorship. And it didn't take long, maybe, maybe about six months, and I was called by The Office of Censorship, and I worked there until 1945 when the war was over. And at that time I decided it was—I was pretty sure by then that what I needed to do was to get a degree in a librarianship. So I went to Columbia, and I was admitted, and I started in Columbia, and I guess it must have been September of '45, graduated in June of '46, and my first job as a librarian was at King's Point. And I went there as an assistant cataloger.

King's Point is to this day the Federal Merchant Marine Academy. Fort Schuyler is the state school for merchant marine studies. At King's Point I was not the only woman professional. The head cataloger, who was a Navy—she had been in the Navy, so she had some expertise with naval personnel and she knew how to handle herself quiet well with them. And they respected her very highly. And I was her assistant, and it was fine. I enjoyed that very much; it was a beginning job. I wasn't being paid much, I think it was something like—oh, I don't know, very little. Because I stayed there for about a year and a half or so, and was offered a job at Hunter College, for what I thought was a monumentally high [laughs] salary, eighteen hundred dollars a year. And the librarian at the time said, "You have to take it, Fil, you can't give that up." And it was head of the catalog department at Hunter College. And even though I was reluctant to leave King's Point, because I enjoyed working there, I liked the atmosphere and everything, and—but I did go to Hunter, and I stayed there about fifteen months because I didn't like the atmosphere [laughs].

But while I was there I met Terry Hoverter. And Terry Hoverter was the librarian at Fort Schuyler, which in those days was called The New York State Nautical School. So he was looking for a cataloger, and he said, "You know I'm going to have a vacancy pretty soon, would you like to consider coming to Fort Schuyler?" and I said, "Yes, I might," and I told him that I had worked at King's Point. And I said it's my understanding that the curriculum is very similar, and I do have cataloging background from King's Point, and also from Hunter. So he said, "Well, why don't you come out for an interview," and so I did that. I went out there in the middle of a snowstorm [laughs] and I thought, "God, I'm never going to do this everyday," because there was no transportation. Fort Schuyler is on a peninsula of Throg's Neck. Throg's Neck is a section of Bronx, New York, and Fort Schuyler is on a peninsula way out into Long Island Sound, really. And we had just had a terrible snowstorm, and I had to walk from where the bus dropped me off to the fort which is easily about close to a mile walk, and in snowdrifts and all of that, and—but I did it, and you know he was happy to see me [laughs] arrive. And we had a nice meeting, and he said, "You know if you want the job you can have it." He said, "I'm really—I really need somebody, and my cataloger is leaving," so I said, "Yes, I'll take it. I'll take it." So we agreed that I would start on March 1st, 1949, which I did.

Now in those days, Fort Schuyler was really a male bastion, and I was coming on as the only professional woman. They had women as clerks, but I was the only professional woman. And the library was manned by the director, Mr. Hoverter, and I was the only other professional person in the library at the time. And I was interested because I was familiar with the book collection; it was very similar to King's Point, and I felt I could handle it without, you know, too much indoctrination. And I thought, "You know, I'll take it." And the most important thing of course was again the salary was higher than I was getting at Hunter. And all these things, you know, made it easy for me to make a decision. So I took it, and I didn't realize what I was really in for. [laughs] But it was okay; as I said I knew what I was getting into, and so I started on March 1st, 1949.

Now I went in with graduate studies. In those days Columbia was not giving you a Master's for the Library Degree, but still it was a graduate degree, I mean it was beyond your baccalaureate. So, I arrived there, and if you check, and this is something that can be checked very easily, if you check the catalogs of the era you will notice that one-third of the faculty at the time had degrees—not degrees—had had their studies only at the schoolship level.

Maritime College started on a schoolship. It started on the *Saint Mary's* in 1874. The *Saint Mary's* was kept until 1908. In 1908 we got the *Newport*, and then these people that I encountered there—and those were two-year courses on the *Saint Mary's* and the *Newport.* They were two-year courses— they were professional courses in seamanship and marine engineering—no academic studies at all. Now a lot of the faculty at that time, one-third, which is a considerable number, one-third of the faculty had their education only on the schoolship—two years. They [laughs] were high and mighty people. And here I am, with much more education, and I was hired as a clerk. Now I questioned that of the librarian at the time, you know. I thought, "Why should I be in the clerical line?" He said, "Well, there's nothing I could do, you know this is the way it is," and you know I accepted. As I said the money was better than I had before, so I took it.

But I didn't realize that these people [laughs] would start treating me like a clerk, and always did, and were mean-spirited about it, you know they really were. I had no restroom facilities. I had to walk two blocks outside of my office. In the winter I had to put on a coat, a hat, and boots to go and wash my hands [laughs]. And these men had—what they used to call them 'heads'—in the navy, a bathroom is a 'head.' They had 'heads' one on top of the other on two separate levels in the fort, and I had to walk two blocks outside, you know, and it was a little ridiculous. I thought that was kind of mean that they couldn't see it my way, but they never did. They just you know continued to—you know—one of—I call—I shouldn't even call them professors, they really weren't, [laughs] but they would come over and throw a piece of paper at me and say, "Type this," you know and I would say, "But, I don't type" —you know [laughs], that kind of thing.

And so I was—I coped with it for thirteen years. Believe it or not, for thirteen years I was in a clerical line. And as I said to Jane earlier, "In a way I think I did an injustice to the profession, not only to myself, but to the profession." Because I wasn't an activist. I really didn't know how to handle those guys. You know macho-ism was exuding [laughs] all over the place, and I just didn't know how to handle it. I used to go home and I used to tell my husband [laughs]—I used to cry on his shoulder, and he used to say, "There's nothing I could do for you. If you can't take it, leave, you don't have to stay there." But I said, "They're not going to run me out. I like my job."

I loved my job. My job was so—was just so fantastic. I went there as a cataloger, but, I took over the duties of government documents. I took over the duties of periodicals. I was the first periodicals librarian. I collected archival material, wherever I could find it. I did all of that. It was so—it was so varied, it was so interesting, I just loved it, and I thought, you know, "I'm not going to let these guys run me out of here, just because they want to treat me as clerk." So the way I handled it was to just ignore them; I just totally ignored them. I had nothing to do with them. I didn't have a single friend on the faculty, and I didn't care, it didn't bother me because I was busy with my work, and happy with my work. And that was really—that was for thirteen years.

Then in nineteen—in the 1960s, I think it was, that The Higher Education Act was passed. I'm not sure exactly what it was called, but it was something like that. And things began to change. But I have to say one other thing; librarians all around the university, all around SUNY, didn't have it much better than me. The only difference was that in my case, on top of not getting equal pay [laughs], for [laughs] for what they doing, there was sex discrimination, really. That's what it really amounted to, and they didn't have that. They didn't have that because you know they didn't have the situation that we did, an all-male faculty.

But in the 1960s then, with The Higher Education Act passed, and things began to change. We got a lot; our budget increased by leaps and bounds. We were able to get much more money to do a lot of things that we were doing by hand. We were writing out the [laughs] catalog card—the subject headings on catalog cards, we were writing them in hand, you know, and now all of a sudden you know we could get printed cards, and so you know it was really—things had—were really changing drastically. And at that time too the librarians all around the university were beginning to feel like maybe they had some clout because there was much more money around, so they formed an association, The State University of New York Library Association, and so of course we were—I felt like I was a charter member of that because I really wanted to get in on something.

And so that began to change things, and I think it was around nineteen—I don't know maybe '61 or '62, we were all told that we could go into a 'professional line,' rather than a clerical line if we wanted to. So again, [laughs] I was called into the office, and the business officer said to me, "You really want to do this? You really want to get out of a clerical line? You have protection as a clerk, you know, civil service protects you," he said, "but if you go into a professional line, you work at the pleasure of the president." And I said, "Well, I don't care. I mean I'm doing my job, I know I'm doing my job, and I'm doing it well, so I'm not afraid of working at the pleasure of the president." So I said, "I'll take my chances." Oh, he was very—you know he really was trying to discourage me. But I think he was doing it—I think he had my best interest at heart, I really believe that. I think he just was afraid that maybe you know the president [laughs] might get up on the wrong side of the bed one day and decide to get rid of a librarian. But anyway I did go along with it, and I went over to the professional line, and that was the end of my stay as a clerk—well I wasn't a clerk, but in a clerical line.

But just to point out some of the—you know mean spirited things that happened at that time. One time, for instance, I had to sit in for the librarian at a meeting where they were expecting a visitor from Albany, and all the department chairs were supposed to attend that meeting, and [Terry] could not go for some reason—he asked me to go. Well I went to the—I knew I was going to be miserable, but I figured I had to go, he asked me to go, and when I get there, [laughs] they all look at me and one of them finally said, "What are you doing here?" And you know I just ignored him. I knew I was going to say the wrong thing, whatever I was going to say, so you know they're looking at each other kind of laughing, and again he said, "What are you doing here?" So I said, "Well, I'm sitting in for Terry," and that's all. I could barely eat. [laughs] I remember that meal; I'll never forget it. [laughs] I could barely eat. I thought this is hard. I don't know what went on at that meeting. Afterwards, when Terry said, "Well, what happened?" I said, "I don't know. I just don't know what happened. I wasn't listening to a thing." [laughs] I was so miserable.

But that was the kind of thing, you know, I had to put up with. And you know I didn't have—as I said we didn't have restroom facilities at all, and it was only because one day we had—we received a gift—and if anybody knows anything about gifts that you get from somebody's attic or basement, it was moldy, and dusty. And I think I had to put on my hat and my coat to go to the restroom, really just to wash my hands, maybe four or five times that day, because the material I was working with was dirty. So that by late afternoon, when I made maybe the fourth trip, I just walked into the admiral's office—because in those days the president of the Maritime College was not called 'president,' he was called, 'admiral' all the time. So I walked into walked into the admiral's office, with my black hands, [laughs] and I held them in his face, and I said, "You know I've made this trip here, maybe four times today, just to wash my hands," and he saw I was practically in tears, so he said, "Sit down, Fil." And so and I explained what happened, I said, "You know we don't have a washroom in the fort for the women." And I said, "that's awful." So he said, "Okay, I'll do something about it." So the next day— was a man of his word, I must say, that was Admiral Durgin— the next day, he came over, he took me into the men's head, and he said, "What if we covered the urinals?" [laughs] So I said, "I don't care what you do. You could leave them just the way they are, just put a latch on the door, and when I'm in there, I'll lock myself in." So he said, "No, we'll fix it up, and this will be your Ladies Room." And he did. So I finally got a ladies room, after two years, after two years, I finally got a ladies room [laughs] which was good [laughs].

Jane: No, this is fine. This is exactly what I wanted to hear and the stories that we need to know about what it was like to be the only woman on campus, I just…

Fil: No, but one of the main things, of course, about library work back then, when you had a small staff, you know a librarian really was a jack of all trades, I don't mean—I mean professionally. As I said, I did everything there, everything, and I was involved in all of the professional collections that we had. And for—even to the very end—but—and the other thing was that when we had a vacancy, when we finally had a vacancy, in—oh, I forgot one very important thing. I started in March of 1949. In June of 1949 Mr. Hoverter hired a reference librarian, but he was male, so he came in as a professional. He came in as a professional. And I questioned that, I said, "You know, Terry, I was here before him." [laughs.]" He said, "There's nothing I could do about it. There's nothing I could do about it." So, Fred O'Hara, was an officer, got a bigger salary, was part of the 'club,' [laughs] was a 'member of the club,' [laughs], and there I was [laughs]—no but that was interesting.

But, I got off the point. I was going to say something else about the work, but—but no it was—it was a real challenge, but as I said, if I didn't enjoy it as much as I did I never—I never could have done it. And only because I have to give my husband a lot of credit, because you know he was—he was really so much support for me. You know as I said he was the only one I could complain to, and he always said, "You don't have to do it. Get out of there if you can't take it." And you know I—but it was really—it really was you know mean, because it wasn't necessary. I wasn't looking for their jobs, you know, and I just wanted, you know, respect. I hate to use that word. It sounds so old-fashioned, but I wanted to be treated the way I thought I should have been treated. And as I said I had more education than one-third of them at least, but they couldn't accept that, they just couldn't. And in those days the school was so military. They all wore uniforms, you know, and so rank was so important to them. You know if you were clerk you were a clerk, and that's all there is to it. You could never aspire [laughs] to be anything else. But that was too bad. That was really too bad.

But, you know, that passed. Like everything else, things change. And in 1973 the college changed totally, because up until then even the student body was all male. And in 1973 we finally got our first female cadets, so things relaxed even a lot more at the college. And you know it was really—it's really a different school than it was when I first started there.

The thing about our library—I really ought to say—put in a plug for the library—the library developed over the years one of the finest maritime collections in the country. We had—that was another thing I enjoy so much—that we had researchers from all over the country corresponding with us, you know looking for information on ships, all kinds of ships, not just ocean-going vessels, but sailing ships as well because our periodicals collection went back to the 1800s, and you know they were so—you know they were so complete that people did—now of course with computers you can get this information anywhere, but it was fun without computers because you know it really brings out the sleuth in you [laughs]. I used to love digging into those things, you know trying to find an elusive fact that they wanted to know about a particular vessel, and we can do it because we had the resources. And after awhile you know people knew that and it was fun to get a phone call asking for me by name, you know because I had done something for somebody else, you know? But it was really great fun. I was sorry when the computers came in. [laughs]

Jane: Now when did they hire other women librarians in the library and what was the …

Fil: In the library? Alvina came in 1969.

Jane: Oh, and she was the first woman in the library?

Fil: She was the first other one.

Jane: And there was faculty rank already at that point? When did you get faculty rank about?

Fil: I would say in the '60's probably.

Jane: So before then it was an all-male, even in the library, except for you?

Fil: Oh, yeah. Oh, yeah.

Jane: I know there were not many library directors, because they lasted for a long time, and they were always ...

Fil: They were—well there were a couple of women upstate, there were a couple of women upstate, but those are the big colleges, you know like Binghamton, and Albany, where they had a staff of you know maybe fifty-sixty people. You know their situation was really entirely different than what we experienced in the little places, you know like Fort Schuyler, where you know as I said—you know for a long time I was the only one.

Jane: Now were you head of reference services, did you...?

Fil: Well—all right I was cataloger for thirteen years. Then when one of the reference librarians left—oh, this is another thing [laughs] that's interesting. When the reference librarian left I asked to—I figured, you know, it would be fun to try something else. So I asked if I could be transferred to be a reference librarian. And let me tell you what he did. [laughs] This was not Mr. Hoverter, this was Dr. Whitten. He went around canvassing all the department chairs, "What would you think if we put Fil Magavero at the reference desk." I mean shouldn't she be behind the scenes as a cataloger for the rest of her life? You know, that kind of thing, that kind of stupidity. You know when I think of it now, nobody else would have taken [laughs] it as long as I did, but I was too chicken. [laughs]. But it's fun to look back on it. You know what? I outlived all of them, that's all I can say. [laughs] They're all gone, [laughs] and I was still there. [laughs]

Jane: But you had a very long commute. You never wanted to…

Fil: I did—no…

Jane: …work in a library closer to home?

Fil: No, and I never got a car either, I never got a car.

Jane: I know that. [laughs]

Fil: No, you know, well I learned what to do on my commute too. I always had something I had—could read, you know, and so no that didn't bother me, I got used to that. But I was always the first one in, I always got there by 7:30, and I was probably always the last one out [laughs]. But, no that was okay, I really loved the job, I really did. And I loved working with the cadets, I really did, I still have people calling me. Just the other day Bill Steffenhagen called me from Oregon, [laughs], and Frank Critelli, from Washington, D.C., calls me. You know I really—I think I helped a lot of them, because in those early years we didn't have—we never—I don't know whether we have a psychiatrist on campus now, but in those days I was certainly not a psychiatrist, but I was an advisor, let me call it that, I was an advisor. I was the only one—they had no liberty during the week, they only had liberty on weekends and only if they didn't have demerits could they leave on a weekend. So they were really tied to the campus, and if they had problems, whether they were physical, financial, social, whatever, they—I knew so many of them well, they worked in the library, or I knew them because I worked with them on research problems, or you know whatever. So they would come and they would tell me their sad tales, and I tried to help them as much as I could, and that was another thing, that was another one of my jobs [laughs], you know but—which I enjoyed doing if I could help them.

Some of them—you know in those days those first—in the '50s—most of those kids were first in their families to go to college, and most of them were from blue-collar families. And I identified with them, I knew exactly where they were coming from. And I thought, "Boy, they need help, they need help." Even if only to listen to them, you know? And in those days too the school was so regimented, it was so military. You know if you were caught cheating it was an automatic dismissal. If you—you know if you told a lie—you know that kind of thing. And I remember one kid, I'll never forget him, his name was Jim Conklin, and he came to me one day and he said, "I have a serious problem." I said, "What?" He said, "The kid next to me in the last exam was cheating." I said, "Are you sure?" He said, "Oh, I'm sure, and I have proof." I said, "What do you mean you have proof?" So he said, "He copied every word from my paper, and I know that because at one point he asked me what a particular word I had written down was." So I said, "Well, Jim, if you have proof, you know what you have to do." He said, "I know, but I don't know if I could do it." He had to turn him in, because if you caught somebody cheating and you didn't turn him in, you were considered as much a cheat. And he said, "If I don't turn him in, I'm going to flunk this course, because how can I prove otherwise that I didn't cheat from him." So, I said,

"Well, I'm not going to tell you what to do, you know what to do, those are the rules."

But you know it was very difficult, and those were the kinds of things that kids needed, they really did, they couldn't go to a teacher because they knew, you know, that they were going to get their 'F' right off the bat, so they needed somebody to kind of you know lead them along. And there were so many other problems. This one kid who was married—they couldn't be married at the time, but this one kid, Joe Cook, was married with a couple of kids. "What am I going to do? I have to make some money, and I have to make the cruise, and I have to go on the cruise, so how am I going to make money to support my family?" And I said, "Well, you can't have it both ways. You're going to either have to ask your family to help you out, or you're going to have to fess up, you're going to have to come out and say what happened." [laughs] You know there was so many of these social problems that they went through, and they were all, you know pretty much—I mean in today's world you'd have to say that they were poor kids, poor, you know financially poor. And this was there first shot as trying to do something good for themselves, and some of them were botching it up, and you know what could you do?

Jane: No, I think The Maritime College is still—has a lot of students like that.

Fil: Oh, I'm sure they do, I'm sure they do.

Jane: One more question? Do we have time. Just kind of to sum up, there were like SUNY—other library associations, and I know you said you talked to your husband when you were having all these problems, did you ever talk to other librarians in other libraries, or in any of these associations about—

Fil: We never had any travel money. I never knew librarians from other campuses in those days. It wasn't until SUNYLA came out [to the Maritime College campus], that was already, thirteen-fifteen years later that I was able to make contact with librarians from other parts of SUNY.

Jane: And do you have any friends in libraries in other parts of New York City, or—

Fil: Oh, yeah, and most of them were in special libraries though, because those are the libraries I dealt with mostly. Our collection, even though we were a four-year college, we dealt with a great many people in the industry, and so our collection, even though we had all of the—all of the necessary English literature, and American literature texts and all of that, our most important collection was what we had in the maritime industry. And so most of the libraries I dealt with were special libraries, and they had different problems entirely. They were considered—you know—like secretaries more, I guess, I don't know, I really don't know, but their collections were really so—so specialized. No it was—as I said it wasn't until the '60s that we really began to mingle with other libraries in SUNY, or CUNY even.

Jane: Well, I think whether on purpose, or by circumstance, you were a pioneering woman in that man's world of a maritime college, and I'm just glad that you were able to...

Fil: [Is laughing] That wonderful world—[laughs]

Jane:—to share all those experiences with us, because although a lot of that still exists there, I think things have—you know—changed.

Fil: I don't know, does it still exist to that extent? I mean, I hope not.

Jane: Not to that extent, no. I certainly didn't have that when I was a librarian there.

Fil: No, it was kind of—yeah—it was foolish, it really was foolish when you think of it.

Story Corps staff member: Do you resent it still? Do you have…

Fil: No I don't. No I don't, because I learned to cope with it, I really did. I turned them off completely, I really did. I really ignored them. They ignored me of course [laughs]. That's how it all started, but I learned how to ignore them too, so it really wasn't—no I didn't resent it. I thought to myself I probably never should have done it knowing I couldn't handle it, you know in a more forceful way—I just didn't know how to do it, and I probably shouldn't have gotten into that. As I said in some ways I feel that maybe I did a disservice to the profession, because had I been—you know more of an activist, had I been more forceful, and—not demanding, but in speaking out about what I wanted, it might have made things easier for other librarians, but I didn't do it.

Jane: Well, that was a tough nut to crack at Maritime, you know.

Fil: Well, it was for me, it really was for me. But as I said I didn't—I never felt like I wanted to leave, because I meant—I don't know whether I said that in the piece, but I think I mentioned it to you, earlier, I never felt that I was harassed physically, I never felt that, I never felt that they were going to [laughs] trip me when I was walking along the street or anything like that. But I did feel that they were—that they were mean, that's the word that really comes to mind all the time. I always used to think, "That's so mean," [laughs], but they were mean, they really were, and they didn't have to be, but...

Jane: But you stayed in touch with so many of them anyway, and you were always very dedicated to...

Fil: Not with them. Not with them, because a lot of them are gone now. But some that—I only made two friends on the faculty really, one was Joe Longobardi, and the other was Norm Wennagel. They were the only two that I really became friendly with, but otherwise I never did make friends with any of them, because I just felt—I really didn't think—if they offered me friendship I really didn't think it was sincere, I think they were just—you know— "Well, let's be nice to Fil, because now she's on the faculty," [laughing] kind of thing. I really didn't think it was friendship. But those two guys were really good.

Jane: And did it change at all when they started hiring female faculty as teachers?

Fil: Well, I don't know. Maybe it did. As I said, I never really got close to any of them. It probably did for some of them. And then you know they had the cruises. That was another thing, and in the early days women weren't allowed to make the cruise. By the time women were allowed to make the cruise I was already in my sixties, you know, so I wasn't going to go on a cruise then. And—but all those things you know that you couldn't do, and you could do, and so—Finito?

Jane: Thank you very much, that was a wonderful group of stories that you told us.

END

BIBLIOGRAPHY

"American Library Directory; a Classified List of Libraries in the United States and Canada, with Personnel and Statistical Data." New York: R.R. Bowker. 1923-.

Andreas, Carol. Sex and Caste in America. Englewood Cliffs: N.J., Prentice-Hall, 1971.

Auerbach, Wanda. "Discrimination against Women in the Academic Library." U. W. [University of Wisconsin] Library News. 17 (1972): 1-11.

Banister, John R. "Just How Right Is Mr. Munn?" Library Journal 75 (1950): 141-45.

Barker, Tommie Dora. "In Reply to the Weaker Sex." Library Journal 63 (1938): 294-96.

Beauvoir, Simone de. The Second Sex. New York: Alfred A. Knopf, 1953.

Brand, Barbara E. "Sex-Typing in Education for Librarianship 1870 - 1920." The Status of Women in Librarianship. Ed. Kathleen M. Heim. New York: Neal-Schuman, 1983. 29-49.

Brouwer, Norman J. Centennial History of the S.U.N.Y. Maritime College at Fort Schuyler, 1874-1974. New York: SUNY Maritime College, 1977.

Brugh, Anne E., and Benjamin R. Beede. "American Librarianship." <u>Signs</u> 1.4 (1976): 943-55.

Bundy, Mary Lee, and Frederick J. Stielow. <u>Activism in American Librarianship, 1962-1973</u>. Contributions in Librarianship and Information Science, No. 58. New York: Greenwood Press, 1987.

Canfield, Ruth. "The ALA Committee on the Status of Women in Librarianship: An Examination of Its History and Impact." Master's Thesis. University of North Carolina at Chapel Hill, 1993.

Caplow, Theodore, and Reece Jerome McGee. <u>The Academic Marketplace</u>. New York: Basic Books, 1958.

Carpenter, Raymond L. and Kenneth Shearer. "Sex and Salary Survey; Selected Statistics of Large Public Libraries in the United States and Canada." <u>Library Journal</u> 97 (1972): 3682-85.

Carson, Pearl G. "The Librarian and the School Faculty." <u>Peabody Journal of Education</u> 7.1 (1929): 13-17.

Cassell, Kay A. "The Women's Rights Struggle in Librarianship: The Task Force on Women." <u>Activism in American Librarianship</u>. Greenwood Press, 1987. 21-29.

Conway, Jill K. <u>Written by Herself : Autobiographies of American Women : An Anthology</u>. 1st ed. New York: Vintage Books, 1992.

Cooper, Michael D. "A Statistical Portrait of Librarians: What the Numbers Say." American Libraries 7.6 (1976): 4.

Cravey, Pamela J. "Occupational Role Identity of Women Academic Librarians." College & Research Libraries 52 (1991): 150-64.

Curtis, Florence. "In Reply to the Weaker Sex." Library Journal 63 (1938): 294.

Cushine, L. "Shh! There Are Great Jobs in the Library." Cosmopolitan 209.1 (1990): 86.

Detlefsen, Ellen Gay, Josephine E. Olson, and Irene Hanson Frieze. "Women & Librarians: Still Too Far Behind." Library Journal 116 (1991): 36-42.

DeVinney, Gemma. "A Chronology of the Faculty Status Movement ; National Movement Leading to SUNY Movement". 1997. (23 October, 2004). 11/7 2005. <http://libweb.lib.buffalo.edu/sw/committees/fec/fcstat_chrono.htm>.

Dewey, Melvil. "Women in Libraries: How They Are Handicapped." Library Notes 1 (1886): 89-92. Reprint of a speech given before the Association of Collegiate Alumnae. In Weibel et. al. pp.10 - 12.

Dowell, David R. "Sex and Salary in a Female Dominated Profession." The Journal of Academic Librarianship 14 (1988): 92-8.

Drills and Exercises, Schoolship "St. Mary's". Videorecording ; Videocassette ; VHS tape Library of Congress], [Washington, D.C., 1995.

"Eight Bells : Yearbook of the New York State Maritime Academy, Fort Schuyler, New York." [New York, N.Y.: The Academy. 1942-.

Fairchild, Mary Salome Cutler. "Women in American Libraries; Originally Published in December 1904." Library Journal 117 (1992): S6 (insert between p32-).

Fisher, William Harvey. "The Question of Gender in Library Management." Library Administration & Management 11 (1997): 231-6.

Frarey, Carlyle J., and Carol L. Learmont. "Placements and Salaries 1974: Promise or Illusion?" Library Journal 100.17 (1975): 1767.

Garrison, Dee. Apostles of Culture : The Public Librarian and American Society, 1876-1920. New York: Macmillan Information, 1979.

Grimm, James W., and Robert N. Stern. "Sex Roles and Internal Labor Market Structures: The "Female" Semi-Professions." Social Problems 21.5 (1974): 690-705.

Grotzinger, Laurel A. "Biographical Research on Women Librarians : Its Paucity, Perils, and Pleasures." The Status of Women in Librarianship : Historical, Sociological, and Economic Issues. Ed. Kathleen M. Heim. New York: Neal-Schuman, 1983. 139-90.

Heilbrun, Carolyn G. Writing a Woman's Life. 1st Ballantine Books ed. New York: Ballantine Books, 1989.

Heim, Kathleen M., and Katherine Phenix. On Account of Sex : An Annotated Bibliography on Women in Librarianship, 1977-1981. Chicago: American Library Association, 1983.

Hildenbrand, Suzanne. "A Historical Perspective on Gender Issues in American Librarianship." The Canadian Journal of Information Science 17 (1992): 18-28.

—. "Revision vs. Reality: Women in the History of the Public Library Movement, 1876-1920." The Status of Women in Librarianship: Historical, Sociological and Economic Issues. Ed. Kathleen M. Heim. New York: Neal-Schuman, 1983. 7-27.

Irvine, Betty Jo. Sex Segregation in Librarianship : Demographic and Career Patterns of Academic Library Administrators. Contributions in Librarianship and Information Science, No. 53. Westport, Conn.: Greenwood Press, 1985.

Ivy, Barbara A. "COSWL & the Future of Women in Librarianship." Library Journal 112 (1987): 42-4.

James, Edward T., and Barbara Sicherman. Notable American Women : A Biographical Dictionary.

Cambridge, Mass.: Belknap Press of Harvard University Press, 1971.

Kaufman, Polly Welts. "The Library in American Culture." History of Education Quarterly 23.1 (1983): 83-89.

Kelly-Gadol, Joan. "Did Women Have a Renaissance?" Becoming Visible: Women in European History. Boston: Houghton Mifflin, 1987. 176-201.

Kelly, Joan. "Early Feminist Theory and the *Querelle Des Femmes*, 1400-1789." Women, History & Theory : The Essays of Joan Kelly. Chicago: University of Chicago Press, 1984. 65-109.

Kessler-Harris, Alice. Out to Work : A History of Wage-Earning Women in the United States. New York: Oxford University Press, 1982.

Lancaster, John Herrold. "Wanted: Librarians!" Peabody Journal of Education 26.3 (1948): 174-76.

Latham, John R. "SLA's 2003 Salary Survey." Information Outlook 7.Issue 11 (2003): 14-19.

Lawton, Kelley Ann. ""This Was a Man's University": The Career of Susan Grey Akers at the University of North Carolina's School of Library Science." Master's University of North Carolina at Chapel Hill, 1995.

"Librarians Get Their Cards." Library Journal 131.Issue 2 (2006): 15-15.

"Librarianship: Erosion or Empowerment?" *Library Personnel News* 6 (1992): 2,5.

Lightfoot, R. M. "Further Discussion." *Library Journal* 63 (1938): 438.

"Losses in Directorships for Women Pegged." *Library Journal* 101 4 (1976): 573.

Magavero, Filomena I. "Personal Interview." 2005.

"Maritime College Accepts 1st Woman." *New York Times* June 29 1972: 43.

Martin, Jean K. "Salary and Position Levels of Females and Males in Academic Libraries." *The Status of Women in Librarianship: Historical, Sociological and Economic Issues.* Ed. Kathleen M. Heim. New York: Neal-Schuman, 1983. 243-85.

Moon, E. "Tokenism at the Top?" *Library Journal* 90 (1965): 4019.

Munn, Ralph. "It Is a Mistake to Recruit Men." *Library Journal* 74 (1949): 1639-40.

NARA, National Archives and Records Administration. "Teaching with Documents: The Civil Rights Act of 1964 and the Equal Employment Opportunity Commission ". March 6, 2006. <http://www.archives.gov/education/lessons/civil-rights-act/>.

Parrish, John B. "Women in Top Level Teaching and Research." AAUW Journal 55 (1962): 106.

Phenix, Katharine. "Sex as a Variable: A Bibliography of Women in Libraries 1975-1985." Library Trends 34 (1985): 169-83.

Phenix, Katharine, Lori A. Goetsch, and Sarah B. Watstein. On Account of Sex: An Annotated Bibliography on the Status of Women in Librarianship, 1982-1986. American Lib. Assn., 1989.

Pritchard, Sarah. M. "The Impact of Feminism on Women in the Profession." Library Journal 114.Issue 13 (1989): 76-77.

Rideing, Willam H. "The Nautical School "St. Marys"." Harper's new monthly magazine 59. 351 (1879): 340-50

Rutzick, Max A. "A Ranking of U.S. Occupations by Earnings." Monthly Labor Review 88.Issue 3 (1965): 249.

Savord, Ruth. "Men vs. Women." Library Journal 63 (1938): 342-43.

Schiller, Anita R. Characteristics of Professional Personnel in College and University Libraries. Urbana: University of Illinois, Library Research Center, 1968.

—. "The Disadvantaged Majority; Women Employed in Libraries." American Libraries 1 (1970): 345-46.

—. Women in Librarianship. Advances in Librarianship. Ed. Melvin J. Voigt. Vol. 4. New York: Academic Press, 1974.

Schuman, Patricia Glass, and Kathleen Weibel. "The Women Arisen." American Libraries 10.Issue 6 (1979): 322-26.

Sicherman, Barbara, and Carol Hurd Green. Notable American Women : The Modern Period : A Biographical Dictionary. Cambridge, Mass.: Belknap Press of Harvard University Press, 1980.

SLA. "SLA Salary Survey." Special Libraries 61.6 (1970).

Tarr, Susan. "The Status of Women in Academic Libraries." North Carolina Libraries 31.Fall (1973): 22-32.

Tuttle, Helen M. W. "Women in Academic Libraries." Library Journal XCVI (1971): 2596.

U.S. Merchant Marine Academy. "History of the United States Merchant Marine Academy". March 9, 2006.
<http://www.usmma.edu/about/History.htm>.

"The Weaker Sex?" Library Journal 63 (1938): 239.

Weibel, Kathleen, Kathleen de la Pena McCook, and Dianne J. Ellsworth. The Role of Women in Librarianship, 1876-1976 : The Entry, Advancement, and Struggle for Equalization in One Profession.

A Neal-Schuman Professional Book. Phoenix: Oryx Press, 1979.

Williamson, Charles C. <u>Training for Library Service; a Report Prepared for the Carnegie Corporation of New York</u>. New York [Updike], 1923.

Woolf, Virginia. <u>A Room of One's Own</u>. New York: London, 1957.

Wooward, Richard B. "At These Landmarks, Shhh Is the Word." <u>The New York Times</u> March 5 2006, sec. Travel Desk: TR3.

"Young Man, Be a Librarian." <u>Esquire</u> 61 (1964): 8.

Young, Mark. "ARL Salary Survey Highlights." <u>ARL: A Bimonthly Report on Research Library Issues & Actions</u>. 240 (2005): 8-9.

ABOUT THE AUTHOR

Jane Brodsky Fitzpatrick is Acquisitions and Collection Development librarian at the City University of New York (CUNY), The Graduate Center. Before working at CUNY, she was Head of Technical Services & Acquisitions at the State University of New York (SUNY) Maritime College in the Bronx, for ten years. She received her MLS at Simmons College in Boston, and a second Master's degree in Liberal Studies at the CUNY Graduate Center.

A native of Massachusetts, in a former life she ran a family art supply and picture framing business in Harvard Square. She has always been interested in women's history. Having listened to Filomena Magavero's unique stories when they both worked at the Maritime College library, Fitzpatrick enrolled in an oral history class, and "Mrs. Magavero" finally agreed to tell her story.

www.ingramcontent.com/pod-product-compliance
Lightning Source LLC
Chambersburg PA
CBHW050916160426
43194CB00011B/2426